OTHER BOOKS BY LUCY FREEMAN

The Beloved Prison

The Severed Soul (with Dr. Herbert S. Strean)

Nightmare (with Emily Peterson and Nancy Lynn Gooch)

The Cry for Love

The Dream

The Case on Cloud Nine

Sparks, The Reflections of a Pioneer Psychoanalyst (with Dr. Karl Menninger)

What do Women Want?

Fight Against Fears

"Before I Kill More"

Psychologist with Gun (with Dr. Harvey Schlossberg)

Betrayal

The Power of Fantasy (with Kerstin Kupfermann)

The Story of Anna O.: The Woman Who Led Freud to Psychoanalysis

Our Wish to Kill: The Murder in All Our Hearts (with Dr. Herbert S. Strean)

HEART'S
WORK

HEART'S WORK

*Civil War Heroine
and Champion of the Mentally Ill,
Dorothea Lynde Dix*

*Charles Schlaifer
and
Lucy Freeman*

PARAGON HOUSE
NEW YORK

First edition, 1991
Published in the United States by
Paragon House
90 Fifth Avenue
New York, NY 10011

Manufactured in the United States of America
10   9   8   7   6   5   4   3   2   1

Library of Congress Cataloging-in-Publication Data

Schlaifer, Charles.
    Heart's work: Civil War heroine and champion of the mentally ill,
Dorothea Lynde Dix/Charles Schlaifer and Lucy Freeman.—1st ed.
        p.   cm.
    Includes index.
    ISBN 1-55778-419-1 : $19.95
    1. Dix, Dorothea Lynde, 1802–1887.   2. Social reformers—
United   States—Biography.   3.   Psychiatric   hospitals—United
States—History—19th century.   I. Freeman, Lucy.   II. Title.
HV28.D6S35   1991
361.92—dc20
[B]   91-10328
                                                                CIP

CONTENTS

ACKNOWLEDGMENTS:

My deepest thanks go to P.J. Dempsey, senior editor, for her valuable suggestions, as well as her appreciation of the herculean achievements of Dorothea Lynde Dix. I also wish to thank Chris O'Connell, assistant editor, for his helpful contributions, and also Edward P. Paige, managing editor of Paragon House.

Profound gratitude also goes to Jane Dystel, literary agent, who also understood the importance of Dorothea Dix's work.

PREFACE

Why did I believe a book about Dorothea Lynde Dix, born at the start of the nineteenth century, would be of interest? My friend and co-author Lucy Freeman and I were talking about a year ago of the history of the mental health movement in the United States. I recalled the magnificent work of Dorothea Lynde Dix, one of the most dramatic, heroic personalities in this field, a woman who had been a heroine to me. Lucy and I realized we had to tell her full story.

I first came across Dorothea's name in 1947, when I was a major factor in the making and promotion of the motion picture *The Snake Pit* and researched mental health history in this country. Her story was a surprise to me, this unsung heroine of the mentally ill and of the Civil War.

In the next few years I devoted myself to helping the mentally ill, in addition to my other work, inspired by Dorothea and the writings of Albert Deutsch and Lucy Freeman and the work of Mary Lasker. It had troubled me over the years why Dorothea Lynde Dix was so unknown, here and abroad. Why was she not a heroine to American women and men, as were Florence Nightingale, English nurse in the Crimean War who was regarded as the founder of modern nursing, and Clara Barton, organizer of the American Red Cross, both of whom were depicted in the movies and books.

I believe the answer is that Dorothea Lynde Dix worked for the mentally ill—from whom society turned its heart and head, so much so that even the four years of her backbreaking work in the Civil War was for the most part forgotten.

Read her story and you too will be proud of this great American woman.

Charles Schlaifer

HEART'S
WORK

1
THE DIE IS CAST

"Women in chains, Dorothea? You saw them?" Dr. William Ellery Channing asked incredulously. Dr. Channing was a prominent minister in Boston who had become a close friend.

"I most certainly did," she replied.

"Then do something about them," Dr. Channing suggested.

She said in her low, soft voice, "But my doctor told me I might have only a year to live." One lung had stopped functioning, and her doctor had warned that she must take life easy if she wanted to keep the other.

Dr. Channing said earnestly, "Make that year do, Dorothea. Remember, everyone needs care and compassion, even the criminals and the insane."

Dorothea Lynde Dix, thirty-nine years old, would make that year "do," and many more to follow. During the years that lay ahead, she would change the thinking of the world in an important area of life.

Several weeks before Dr. Channing's suggestion, on a snowy windy Sunday, March 28, 1841, Dorothea walked the few blocks to her church, as she did every week. When the services ended, she drew her cloth coat tightly over her slim form and left the church, once more to battle the heavy snow and a violent wind that threatened to destroy her umbrella.

Two men walked behind her, talking in loud indignant voices. They were condemning the unspeakable conditions of the many insane men and women who were forced to exist in dark caverns beneath Boston's East Cambridge Jail.

"We *must* do something to rescue these tortured souls," said one of the men earnestly.

Then they turned down a block and walked away from her. After she entered her room in the boardinghouse, as she took off her wet coat and shoes she thought of those unfortunates described by the one man as "tortured souls." She felt deeply moved by his words; they were about to change her life from a kind of nothingness to great accomplishments. She felt herself responding to his plea as though it were an order.

Until the last five years of her recuperation, after falling ill with severe tuberculosis, Dorothea had been a highly successful teacher in the two private schools she had established for young pupils. She had collapsed in class one day, and the doctor ordered her to cease all teaching at once. He told her grimly that she needed to rest for a few years if she wanted to stay alive.

Luckily Dorothea could financially afford to do so. She had earned money teaching since she was fifteen. She also had received a large inheritance from her recently deceased, wealthy grandmother, with whom she had lived since the age of twelve. She felt ready for an important change in her life.

A few days before the two men of the snowstorm had deplored the horrendous conditions under which the insane poor of Boston were forced to live, Dorothea's landlady informed her she had a caller. Dorothea welcomed the Reverend John T. G. Nichols, a thin, earnest young man. He was the son of a woman Dorothea had known when she lived with her grandmother at nearby Dix Mansion, a large stately house.

The Reverend Nichols appealed to Dorothea for help, not realizing that he was about to set in motion thoughts within her that would benefit hundreds of thousands of those in need of a caring society.

He explained that he had started to teach the Bible to a group of women who had been jailed for various unlawful acts, but that they refused to pay attention to a man.

He asked Dorothea if she would be willing to take his place for a few Sunday mornings at the Middlesex County House of Correction, known as the East Cambridge Jail. She had long wanted to explore the jail and quickly agreed to take the Reverend Nichols's place. The following Sunday she rode via horse and carriage the few miles to the jail, located in a swampy area in East Cambridge. The corridors, as she walked down them with the jailer, were damp and smelled like stale mutton.

The jailer left her at one large cell where a dozen women prisoners were confined. After she listened to the woes of the women, who insisted they were innocent and complained of the "terrible" food, she asked the jailer, "Will you take me to where the insane are kept?"

"Why do you want to know?" He looked at her suspiciously.

She said quietly, "I'd like to see them."

"No stranger is allowed in that area," he retorted.

"I don't understand why they are there," she said. "They committed no crime. They only lost their minds."

He looked at her intently, his eyes suddenly softened, perhaps feeling a moment of pity for the insane. Then he ordered, "Follow me."

He led her past rows of cells that looked down on the gallows, past the scaffold where the murderous guilty were hung, then out into the prison yard.

At the edge of one of several wooden buildings, he lifted up a heavy trap door. He motioned her to follow him down mouldy steps into a black cavern filled with the chill of the swamps. He lit a lantern, and it illuminated a thick stone pier that ran the full length of the cavern. Each side contained a row of black rusty iron doors.

He explained that these cells, distant from the rest of the jail, had once been used for the solitary confinement of murderers. But now the county kept its "indigent insane" in them, so prisoners who had committed crimes would not be kept awake all night by the unearthly cries and screams of the "crazies."

The jailer walked along the stone pier, opening door after door. Dorothea's senses took in obscene odors and heard agonized shrieks of pain. Finally he opened one door wide, holding up the lantern to illuminate the dark. A few feet away, Dorothea glimpsed two emaciated women lying on filthy straw, wearing rags. They were chained to the wall, penned sideways in coops made of slats. One was old and toothless, with streaming unkempt white hair. She was screaming a string of nonsensical words.

Moved by a sudden deep flow of pity, Dorothea knelt beside the old woman. She gently touched the bony shoulder as though to comfort her. The woman stopped her screams. She turned fierce dark eyes filled with suspicion on Dorothea and stared into her blue eyes. Suddenly the woman's eyes filled with tears.

Dorothea noticed that the room was ice cold; she was shivering though she wore her coat. There was no stove, no means of keeping warm. She asked the jailer what happened to the heat. He told her, "These people don't need a fire. It wouldn't be safe for them. They'd burn themselves up."

She felt sudden anger at the thought that those who were already suffering acutely because of disturbances of the mind, not because of any criminal deed, were subjected to the further punishment of freezing to death in subzero temperature.

Dorothea decided she had seen enough for one day. She thanked the jailer for giving her his time. After she returned to her apartment, she thought of the unbelievable torture endured by innocent men and women who had committed no crime against society. She made up her mind at once as to her next step on that snowy Sunday when the man said, "We *must* do something to rescue these tortured souls."

She now wanted to find out if the conditions in the East Cambridge Jail were an exception or the rule throughout the state of Massachusetts. Notebook in hand, she started her exploration. For the next two years, she would visit every jail and almshouse, from Berkshire in the west to Cape Cod in the east as she accumulated a mass of eyewitness testimony that "shocked and appalled her," according to Francis Tiffany, who wrote *Life of Dorothea Dix* published in 1891 by the Riverside Press in Cambridge, Massachusetts.

Before Dorothea started on her mission, she again consulted Dr. Channing in his home on Mount Vernon Street near the state cap-

The Die Is Cast 5

itol. She described the horrors at the East Cambridge Jail, spoke of
the inhumanity of man to man. She asked her minister what she
could do to help the insane poor.

He suggested that she arouse public opinion and gave the names
of three of his parishioners who might advise her: Horace Mann, a
legislator in the Massachusetts Assembly, who believed every child
in America should have a free education; Dr. Charles Sumner, whose
speeches against slavery had stirred the pity of thousands; and Dr.
Samuel Gridley Howe, head of the Perkins Institute for the Blind
and of the State Board of Education. These men were known as the
"three horsemen of reform" in Massachusetts.

Dorothea called first on Dr. Howe, whose institute was housed in
a converted hotel in South Boston. She knew he had recently appeared before the legislatures of seventeen states to plead the cause
of the blind.

She described to him the horrors she had seen in the East Cambridge Jail, where the mentally ill were chained and mistreated. She
said she wanted to work in their behalf but did not know where to
start and was asking him to tell her the way. He agreed to give her
the names of other jails in which the insane were confined.

When she saw Dr. Sumner in his office at Harvard, where he
lectured on jurisprudence, he told her that Dr. Howe had called on
him in her behalf and he would do what he could to help her. He said
he and Dr. Howe would visit some of the Massachusetts prisons and
report on them.

She then visited the third man, Horace Mann, the head of the
State Board of Education. She asked him why there was no hospital
in Boston for the indigent insane. He told her that the state legislature would not vote money even for a survey.

Dorothea suggested that the legislature be educated, convinced of
the drastic need for ways in which the insane could be helped, not
made more grotesquely ill. Mann asked her how to accomplish this
task. She proposed that a private person make a statewide survey,
incurring the cost. He then asked if she knew what it would mean to
visit every jail, workhouse, and almshouse in the state.

He asked further if she could think of any man in his right mind
who would undertake such a survey. She replied she did not say
"man" but a "woman" might. He looked at her in amazement. A few

days later she started her survey of Massachusetts prisons, after she was given their locations by Mann.

Dorothea traveled from town to town, finding the roads that led to the jails and poorhouses. She also located the indigent insane in barns, sheds, and stalls. In Shelburne, on the Connecticut River in the western part of the state, she discovered a man in a cage being fed like an animal, his food thrown to him on the floor. When she asked the jailer why the man was not given a plate, the reply was, "It's all the same to him how he eats."

In Newton, not far from Boston, she found the worst case of suffering she had yet seen. An old man tied with chains lay in a crib filled with straw. From the straw protruded not legs but stumps. The jailer explained that the old man had been "farmed out" by the town and the farmer who took him in had forgotten his existence one night, leaving him in a freezing-cold shed. The bottom of the old man's legs had frozen, and he was returned to the care of the town; he now lived in a barn behind the almshouse.

When Dorothea asked why he was kept chained, since he could not walk, she was told "he might crawl around and do some damage." In her notebook she wrote, "The keepers have to be educated. Familiarity with suffering may blunt sensibilities. Where neglect once takes a footing other injuries are multiplied."

For the next year and a half, Dorothea traveled all over the state by coach, train, and swaying canal boat. She slept in taverns and farmhouses. Everywhere she stopped, she found the same indifference to human suffering. At first, she felt anger; then she told herself she had to learn to be temperate.

When she returned to Boston, her portmanteau was heavy with black notebooks. She had visited almost five hundred towns, recording the suffering of a thousand insane men and women who were unable to support themselves.

Six months after her first visit to the East Cambridge Jail, Dr. Howe kept his promise to do something about her plea. He wrote an article on September 8, 1841, backing her research. The article, published in the Boston *Daily Advertiser*, fiercely attacked the abuses of the mentally ill in jails and said that the sufferings he had seen were "not fit for our time."

Then a letter by Dr. Sumner to Dr. Howe, written September 8,

1841 appeared in the *Daily Advertiser*; it contained the words: "My dear Howe: All that was reported of the East Cambridge Jail is true. I have been there. I have seen all that you have seen. Let me write of one case."

Dr. Sumner described "two women in coops, one furiously mad, screaming vilest imprecations all day; the other slightly melancholy, her reason scarcely clouded. In this way, in heathen times, the dead were sometimes tied to the living, the cruelest of all punishments. Such horrors I saw in the East Cambridge Jail."

He thanked Dr. Howe for presenting "*a true picture* of the conditions in which unfortunates were cramped together in rooms poorly ventilated and noisome, with filth. You cannot forget the small room in which was confined the raving maniac, from whom long since reason had fled, never to return."

People read this description and were shocked. Letters flooded the columns of the *Boston Advertiser*, protesting such conditions. The county commissioners voted at once to install a stove in the basement of the East Cambridge Jail to give heat "to the insane housed now in the cells of solitary confinement."

These letters marked the start of a life in which Dorothea would be championed by men at the top who helped her change the treatment of the mentally ill from total neglect to a more humane way of existence. She started her work in Boston, but before she was finished, it circled much of the world.

She also studied the most advanced methods of that time in the humane and scientific treatment of insanity. She sought the help of important men in charge of the few asylums for the rich in Boston. These men included Dr. Samuel Woodward, director of the Worcester State Hospital; Dr. Luther V. Bell, director of what at first was called the McLean Asylum, and Dr. John S. Butler, superintendent of the newly erected Lunatic Hospital of Boston.

Dorothea became Dr. Butler's pupil, witnessing with her own eyes the transformation of the brutal madhouse of the past into a humane retreat where the mentally ill were helped to regain their sanity.

In 1843, two years after her first visit to the East Cambridge Jail, Dorothea presented her findings, *A Memorial to the Massachusetts Legislature* in writing. She wrote in part:

Gentlemen . . . About two years since, leisure afforded opportunity, and duty prompted me, to visit several prisons and almshouses in the vicinity of this metropolis. . . . Every investigation has given depth to the conviction that it is only by decided, prompt, and vigorous legislation that the evils to which I refer, and which I shall proceed more fully to illustrate, can be remedied.

I shall be obliged to speak with great plainness, and to reveal many things revolting to the taste, and from which my woman's nature shrinks with peculiar sensitiveness. But truth is the highest consideration. I tell what I have seen, *painful and shocking as the details often are, that from them you may feel more deeply the imperative obligation which lies upon you to prevent the possibility of a repetition or continuance of such outrages upon humanity.*

If my pictures are displeasing, coarse and severe, my subjects, it must be recollected, offer no tranquil, refining, or composing features. The condition of human beings reduced to the extremest state of degradation and misery cannot be exhibited in softened language, or adorn a polished page.

I proceed, gentlemen, briefly to call your attention to the present *state of insane persons confined within this Commonwealth, in* cages, closets, cellars, stalls, pens; chained, naked, beaten with rods, *and* lashed into obedience!

She gave a few illustrations, saying "description fades before reality":

Danvers. *November. Visited the almshouse . . . here are from fifty-six to sixty inmates: one idiotic; three insane; one of the latter in close confinement at all times. Long before reaching the house, wild shouts, snatches of rude songs, imprecations and obscene languages, fell upon the ear. . . . Found the mistress, and was conducted to the place which was then called* "the home" *of the forlorn maniac, a young woman exhibiting a condition of neglect and misery blotting out the faintest idea of comfort and outraging every sentiment of decency.*

She had been, I learnt, a respectable person, industrious and worthy; disappointments and trials shook her mind, and finally laid prostrate reason and self-controls; she became a maniac for life! . . . She had passed from one degree of violence and degradation to another. . . . There she stood, with naked arms and disheveled hair; the un- washed frame invested with fragments of unclean gar- ments; the air so extremely offensive though ventilation was afforded on all sides save one, that it was not possible to remain beyond a few moments without retreating for recovery to the outward air. Irritation of body, produced by utter filth and exposure, incited her to the horrid pro- cess of tearing off her skin by inches; her face, neck and person were thus disfigured to hideousness.

Dorothea added, "Some may say these things cannot be re- medied; these furious maniacs are not to be raised from these base conditions. I *know* they are; could give *many* examples," and pro- ceeded to tell of a young woman who was for years "a raging maniac," chained in a cage and whipped to control her acts and words. She was helped by a husband and wife who agreed to take care of her in their home. Slowly she recovered her senses.

Dorothea then described the case of a young man who had been declared "incurably insane" and thrown into a poorhouse, chained in an iron collar. Visiting him the preceding June, she found him sitting in darkness and alone, as he did for weeks, unable to speak. She went on with case after case of men and women of all ages who were chained and "almost or quite sunk into a state of dementia." She spoke of these trapped unhappy prisoners as suffering "from loneli- ness and heart-hunger."

Dr. Howe addressed the legislature on February 2. He said, "Gentlemen, I move for resolves on the hospital bill. I move we vote two hundred thousand dollars to build an addition to the state hospital for the insane at Worcester. Two hundred applications to the state hospital are rejected each year for lack of room. A thousand insane lie in attics and cellars!"

The next day the legislature passed the bill. According to a man named Baker, who found a letter Dorothea had written to Horace Mann, thanking him for his support, she wrote: "Dear Friend, in all my efforts to help the suffering, I have only followed in the footpaths you have trodden." She spoke of Mann's achievement in having paved the way for suffering men and women by creating the Worcester State Hospital, to which her efforts would only add.

She also mentioned Mann's great achievement for free education, the building of schools to train teachers, the creation of schools that would teach poor and rich alike. Praising his work, she said, "I know that the usages of society crush free and cordial friendship, and silence the expression of actual truehearted sympathy. And to reveal the united sentiments of the heart and mind is almost as infrequent as to find hearts to cherish and minds to enshrine."

On his part, Mann wrote, "For her thoughts on prisons alone, Dorothea Lynde Dix is entitled to a place in history."

Dorothea had a way with words—her father had taught her early to read and write and to enjoy the language of the centuries. She could with ease appeal to the men at the top, who then helped her change the treatment of the mentally ill who did not possess funds.

Who was this amazing woman, gifted with an unbelievable courage that enabled her to appeal to the men who ruled the nation, which at this time reached only to the Mississippi River? Dorothea would address other legislatures, including the Congress of the United States, national legislative bodies in England and in many of the countries of Europe, spurring them to provide adequate facilities for their insane or "mentally disturbed," as they were later more humanely identified.

What drove Dorothea Lynde Dix to her often-dangerous but challenging mission? It was unheard of in the United States at this time for a woman to embark on such missions. What created her dedication, a resolute one, her pursuit of decent quarters for the "insane?"

She did not have to subject herself to the perils she undertook, both physical and emotional, but could have lived in Boston comfortably, financially well off.

Why could Dorothea not settle for a safer, more quiet existence, as most other women did? What caused her now lifelong dedication to the unfortunate men and women who temporarily had lost their minds and were without anyone to help them regain their sanity?

2
"I NEVER KNEW CHILDHOOD"

Dorothea Lynde Dix, her parents' first child, was born April 4, 1802, in the town of Hampden on the Penobscot River in Maine. Hampden was one of the many places in which, according to Tiffany, her father Joseph, "who was of an unstable and wandering turn of mind," would live.

Joseph had entered Harvard University at seventeen, angering his father by suddenly forsaking his parents' Calvinist fervor and turning to the teachings of the preacher Charles Wesley. The latter wandered the streets bringing faith in God to the poor. After Joseph's parents showed their disgust at this championing of Wesley, Joseph began to drink in Boston taverns.

When he was eighteen, Joseph fell in love with Mary Bigelow, who was eighteen years older than he. He married her in spite of his parents' strong objections. The date of their marriage remains unknown. He was then expelled from Harvard, which had a rule that no student could marry and remain in college.

It was then that Dr. Elijah Dix dispatched his son and his son's new wife to Hampden, believing that Joseph could act as a land agent for valuable property Dr. Dix had bought. But Joseph was not interested in the sale of land; he wanted only to write of salvation of the spirit, following the practice of Charles Wesley.

At times Joseph appeared emotionally unbalanced as his uncertain behavior showed. On the one hand, he was a minister, and on the other hand, he drank heavily. Among what Tiffany described as the "abnormal tendencies" of Dorothea's father "was one of subjection to states of fanatical religious excitement, during which he became wholly engrossed in writing and issuing tracts, the supreme importance of which to the world's salvation outweighed in his mind every question of the material maintenance and needful education of his family."

Neither Joseph nor Mary could meet the arduous demands of the frontier life in Maine, especially after two more children were born. Their son Joseph arrived when Dorothea was four, followed by Charles Wesley, whose date of birth is not known, named after the preacher his father idolized.

Before Hampden was taken by the British in the War of 1812, Joseph and his family took refuge in Worcester, Massachusetts. There Dorothea helped her father paste and stitch together his religious tracts. Tiffany described her as a proud, ambitious, and high-spirited girl who sought refuge at her grandparents' large home in Boston when her parents fought. If her father drank too heavily, he would at times strike her mother.

Dorothea's grandfather was an influential figure. Dr. Dix was born August 24, 1747, in Watertown, Massachusetts, of early New England settlers. He did not have the money to go to college in Worcester, where he was brought up, but he studied the practice of medicine for three years in Boston under Dr. William Greenleaf, with whom he worked in an office for sixteen years. By 1775 Dr. Dix had established a drug store on the south side of Faneuil Hall. He also found chemical ways of refining sulphur and purifying camphor.

Dr. Dix married Dorothy Lynde, then twenty-five, on October 1, 1771, before the outbreak of the Revolutionary War. Dorothy, the eighth of seventeen children, was known as the "belle of Worcester." Her father, Joseph Lynde, was a graduate of Harvard and very wealthy. After the burning of Charlestown, Massachusetts by British troops, he sought refuge in Worcester for his wife and children. Tiffany described Madame Dix as "a typical example of the New England Puritan gentlewoman of the period—dignified, precise, inflexibly conscientious, unimaginative, and without a trace of emotional glow or charm."

Dr. Dix and his wife had seven sons and one daughter, according to Helen E. Marshall in *Dorothea Lynde Dix: Forgotten Samaritan*, published in 1937 by the University of North Carolina Press. Marshall deplored the fact that the name of Dorothea Lynde Dix somehow "has been all but lost to posterity."

William, the oldest son, was born August 2, 1772, followed by Joseph, on February 6, 1774, who died shortly afterward (no date given). The only girl, Mary, was born April 14, 1776; another "Joseph," to replace his dead brother, was born March 29, 1778; Clarendon was born September 26, 1779, John was born April 1, 1781; and Henry Elijah was born February 6, 1793. No date is given for Alexander, the seventh son.

Marshall wrote that three sons were "victims of their own vices and suffered early, tragic deaths." William Dix, the eldest, died in Dominica, West Indies, in 1799; Alexander, the sixth son, was killed in Canada on March 23, 1809; and Clarendon, the fourth son, lost his life in Kentucky on September 1, 1811.

The salient traits of Dr. Dix's character, according to Tiffany, were indomitable energy, a spirit of initiative in new enterprises, a fertility of resources, dogged honesty, a large public spirit, and a "masterful temperament that would ride over obstacles, no matter at what cost of personal popularity." These same traits would be found in his granddaughter, who absorbed them from him.

Dorothea was only seven when Dr. Dix died on June 7, 1809, during a visit to Dixmont Centre, Maine. His body was interred there in the burial ground. Dorothea always retained a vivid remembrance of him, aware that he had been openly fond of her. He insisted, when she visited, that she drive around with him in his carriage as he talked to her "in his strong and racy way," in Tiffany's description. Her grandfather seemed to stand out as the one bright spot in her earliest memories. He implanted in her mind a lifelong admiration for his friendly, admirable qualities. She remembered him as a tall man who wore white garters and a broad-brimmed hat when he went out.

Her grandparents lived in a stately redbrick house on Orange Court that boasted a tall cupola and five glass windows. It was furnished with expensive chairs, tables, desks, bureaus, poster beds, and luxurious carpets. In all, it was a magnificent home, in contrast to the cabins in which Dorothea grew up. She had lived in crude, small log houses where heavy shutters kept out the cold and a fireplace was used for heating, cooking, ventilation, and lighting. The furniture was homemade, as were the chests, tables, beds, chairs, and benches.

Dr. Dix delighted in leading his little blue-eyed granddaughter, who no doubt reminded him of his daughter, Mary, now married to the Reverend Thaddeus Mason Harris, pastor of the Old Meeting House Hill Church in Dorchester, into the huge flower garden in the rear of Dix Mansion. He would point out the beds of phlox, marigolds, astors, tiger lilies, and hollyhocks that bloomed in spring and summer. One chance seed that suddenly sprung to life became known as the Dix pear. The myriad flowers awakened in Dorothea an everlasting love of nature that she never lost, since she associated their beauty with her beloved grandfather.

Tiffany described this house, in which Dorothea lived after age twelve, as a "grim and joyless home, but none the less it was a home in which she was trained to habits of unremitting diligence." She felt grateful to her somewhat emotionally detached grandmother for providing shelter, food, and a modicum of caring at a time when she desperately needed it. Madame Dix once had been active bringing up her sons and daughter. She welcomed company to her lonely house after the death of her husband, whom she survived by twenty-eight years, and the vanishing of most of her sons.

According to Rachel Baker, whose *Angel of Mercy* was published by Julian Mesner in 1955, and whose daughter Joanna Baker did much of the research, Dorothea's grandmother had dark hair, often wore a cameo on a black ribbon around her neck, and embroidered fine linen. The windows of the parlor boasted velvet curtains, and a silver tea service adorned the corner table.

At times of trouble in the log cabins, Dorothea's parents would send her by carriage to her grandparents' house. Dorothea passed the first seven years of her life between the small cottage in Hampden and the large house on Orange Court in Boston. In summer 1809, when she was seven, Dorothea stayed with her grandparents for seven weeks, according to Baker. There was always action in Boston. Her grandfather would drive her to the docks to see the loads of chemicals being shipped to England from his factory in South Boston, one of his many enterprises. He also enjoyed walking with her to the large stable behind Dix Mansion where, smiling and happy, she stroked the soft noses of his carriage horses.

Grandparents often have a strong influence on the lives of their grandchildren, especially when they make the grandchildren feel loved and wanted, something parents may not consistently do. It is revealing of her love for her grandfather that, of the many asylums for the indigent insane that Dorothea later helped found, the only one she permitted to be associated with her family name was Dixmont Hospital in Pennsylvania, which she thought of as a memorial to her grandfather.

Soon after the loss of her grandfather, Dorothea, her parents, and two brothers moved from Hampden to the village of Bernard in Vermont, where they lived in another small cottage. Dorothea's grandmother had written saying she wanted nothing more to do with her late husband's project in Maine, and it collapsed. In the new home, Dorothea acted as a messenger for her father, going from cottage to cottage and dispersing handbills that announced, "Books from Boston sold at cheap prices. Farm vegetables and produce taken in exchange," according to Baker's description of Joseph's attempts to earn a living.

Joseph kept special books in what he called his "Harvard box," cherishing the knowledge he had acquired in his year and a half at college. He allowed no one to touch the books except his daughter. He taught her to read and she learned to love words from him. When she first went to school, she wrote much faster than the other children. She also taught her brothers Joseph and Charles Wesley to read and write.

Dorothea's parents soon moved to Worcester and lived in still another cottage at the edge of town, Tiffany wrote. Joseph was now drinking heavily, and Dorothea's mother suffered from acute, incurable headaches, unable to do much work around the house or to care for her daughter and two younger sons.

Madame Dix was now living alone, and she conferred with Judge Bangs, Dorothea's great-uncle on her grandmother's side, and her sister, Sarah Duncan, who lived in Worcester. It was decided that Madame Dix would look after Dorothea and her two brothers; she invited them to stay with her at Dix Mansion. Dorothea's parents were taken in a carriage to New Hampsted, to board with a distant relative of Dorothea's mother, who agreed to look after the two needy parents for a fee, paid by Madame Dix.

Dorothea was twelve, Madame Dix was seventy. Madame Dix sent Joseph to Latin School and paid a nurse to care for little Charles Wesley. She insisted that Dorothea, whose dark hair now drooped over her blue eyes, wear her hair back and over her ears. She also encouraged Dorothea to learn to "stand up straight and walk properly," hold her head high.

Madame Dix hoped her granddaughter in a few years would be a "belle," as she had been in her teens, and available for marriage. She hired a dancing instructor and a seamstress who fashioned new clothes for Dorothea, who had arrived with only a well-worn calico dress, all her parents could afford.

Dorothea showed little desire to dance or to become a "belle." She wanted to feed the beggar children at the gate (starved, as she must have felt at the times her father had no money). She was interested not in acquiring clothes, but in helping the needy, as her father had been.

When Dorothea was fourteen, her grandmother sent for her sister Sarah and asked her to help decide what could be done for this stubborn adolescent who did not want to dress up and seek a suitable husband. Mrs. Duncan, who had always loved Dorothy, offered to take her into her home for a while and see what progress she could make. This "while" would last almost four years.

Once in Worcester, Dorothea reluctantly appeared at parties her rich relatives held regularly, many at her aunt and uncle's large home. There she met her second cousin, Edward Bangs, a tall, handsome man, an attorney, fourteen years older. Edward, at once attracted to his younger second cousin, appeared frequently at tea-time. He sought Dorothea out, asking about her life. For a young man, he had climbed high in politics and worked with General Levi Lincoln who, it was predicted, would someday be governor of Massachusetts.

Edward asked Dorothea what she wanted to do with her life. She told him she wished to become a schoolteacher, that she enjoyed telling stories to entertain little girls. He suggested that she start what was called "a little dame school." She asked what he meant.

He explained that girls were not permitted to attend public schools in Boston at this time (the law was changed in 1890). The girls could, however, be taught privately by young women, usually in the latter's home or in the back room of a store. He told Dorothea that many rich families would welcome a "little dame school" where their daughters, and their sons if they wished, could learn to read. He offered to find pupils for her and quarters in which she could teach.

He located a room over a bookstore on Main Street. Dorothea faced her first pupils at age fifteen (not including the "pupils" who had been her brothers in earlier years). The new pupils were between six and eight years old. She held her first class in autumn 1816—six girls and three boys appeared, according to Baker. She told them stories of the wonders of nature, including how rocks were shaped, how flowers grew, and how the light of the Milky Way streamed down from heaven. She also started to keep notes in a book she called "Conversations on Common Things."

Edward visited her often, and no doubt she felt grateful for his suggesting that she teach. She spent three years with her pupils in Worcester, since her aunt highly approved of the venture. Twenty pupils, both boys and girls, attended the first year.

One afternoon when she was eighteen, Edward walked her home from the store, as he frequently did. He told her he had fallen in love with her and wanted to marry her. He was now thirty-one. Frightened at the thought of marriage, remembering the rocky marriage of her parents, Dorothea ran into the house. The next day she closed the school and returned to her grandmother in Boston, according to Baker.

Her grandmother, now almost seventy-five, welcomed her and noted with satisfaction changes in her dress, which was far more sophisticated. Edward wrote loving letters. One day in the spring he appeared and proposed to her again in her grandmother's garden of pear trees and flowers. This time Dorothea did not feel so awed and afraid. She allowed him to present her with a ring, but refused to set a date for marriage. She evidently liked him very much, was grateful for his help in starting her on a career of teaching, but dreaded the thought of marriage—it meant desertion of children, emotional outbreaks, fights, heavy drinking. This would be the only time in her life that she would even consider marrying.

She had been excited and pleased with the work involved in teaching at Worcester. She now took another important step. She subscribed to public lectures given by Harvard professors, read all her grandfather's erudite books, and haunted the libraries in Boston.

Marshall summed it up: "She had left Boston an impetuous, willful child; she returned an eager, ambitious young woman, a trifle dictatorial but with a growing personal magnetism and modest charm. Dorothea Dix would always have her way in life, but in the schoolroom at Worcester she had acquired something of a technique by which she obtained her end without becoming obnoxious."

Not daring to ask her grandmother outright, she wrote a letter requesting permission to teach two different types of children at Dix Mansion, pointing out that little girls were denied all chance to attend school unless it was held in a private home or store. She no doubt felt she could express her desires more eloquently on paper than face to face with this often difficult woman.

The letter described the first type of children. It read:

> *My Dear Grandmother,—Had I the saint-like eloquence of our minister, I would employ it in explaining all the motives, and dwelling on all the good, good to the poor, the miserable, the idle, and the ignorant, which would follow your giving me permission to use the barn chamber for a school-room for charitable and religious purposes. You have read Hannah More's life, you approve of her labors*

for the most degraded of England's paupers; why not, when it can be done without exposure or expense, let me rescue some of America's miserable children, from vice and guilt?

Do my dear grandmother, yield to my request, and witness next summer the reward of your benevolent and Christian compliance.

Your affectionate Granddaughter,

D. L. Dix.

A second letter followed with the request that she also be allowed to establish another school within the Dix Mansion for children of wealthy parents, chiefly girls. She believed that both the rich and the poor deserved a chance to acquire knowledge early in life.

To her deep relief, her grandmother gave her permission for both schools to be conducted on her land. She showed that in spite of her strong wish that Dorothea marry and raise a family, she was willing to encourage Dorothea in her chosen work, even though it was highly unusual for a woman in this era to select any profession. Madame Dix's immediate consent speaks of her ability to overcome her usual rigidity of mind at times.

The support of her grandmother played an important role in the rest of Dorothea's life. Her grandmother's sanctioning of Dorothea's choice of a profession gave her even more courage to carry through whatever she wanted to tackle to help make the world a better place.

Though she no doubt had mourned at twelve, when she had to leave her unstable parents to live with her sometimes icelike grandmother, she could now feel "special." Thereafter she was always grateful to her grandmother for understanding and supporting her vital desire to be a teacher. One might say, in a sense, that she would later in another area become one of the greatest teachers of all time.

As Dorothea started her "little dames" schools in Boston on April 2, 1821, just before her nineteenth birthday, she received the tragic news that her father had died in New Hampshire. There was no report that the cause of death was alcoholism, but his excessive drinking over the years no doubt had affected his body.

Though Dorothea had seen little of her father since she was twelve, she would never forget the many ways he had helped her gain a sense of herself through books, new ideas, and the love of poetry.

Edward was still seeking her as his wife, but when she next saw him, she handed him the engagement ring and told him she could not marry him. He pleaded with her, saying she was upset because of her father's death and insisting that he would wait for her to change her mind.

She had set her goal, she had educated herself for a career that would support her financially, bring her respect, and was in an area that she enjoyed studying. She had also become a child-mother to her two younger brothers since they, too, lived under their grandmother's roof.

Dorothea realized that her parents had been emotionally and financially unable to raise three children. It was all her mother, a neurotic woman, always ill, could do to care for her husband, much less her offspring. No mention is made by Tiffany, Baker, or Marshall of whether Dorothea ever saw her mother again. Perhaps she did not because of Madame Dix's open hatred of Mary Dix. Dorothea, after all, had been named for her father's mother, not her own mother.

Dorothea wanted her brothers to be educated fully so they could earn money for their future families, unlike their father, who had never been a success at any kind of work. Joseph would finish attending the Boston Latin School in 1832 and become a prosperous merchant in Boston. Charles Wesley, the younger son, "a strange, silent boy," according to Tiffany, ran off to sea and died on the Western coast of Africa aboard a ship he commanded.

Dorothea owed her grandmother a debt of lasting obligation in allowing her to live and teach at the mansion, even if it had proved a cold atmosphere in which to grow up, "a grim and loveless home," in Tiffany's words. She was not allowed to misplace a particle in a sentence, as much a sin in her grandmother's eyes as a misplaced stitch in a shirt. But at least it was the secure "home" that Dorothea felt her mother and father had never provided.

Dorothea now acquired a house in which to live permanently if she wished. Her grandmother had given her shelter and an education even though she had never offered loving arms in which to nestle or a sympathetic mind that would listen to Dorothea's most troublesome thoughts. In later years, Dorothea would say, "I never knew childhood!"

When she left Worcester to return to Dix Mansion, she tried at first to act as her grandmother requested: pay attention to clothes and look for a husband. But Dorothea's desire to teach, to expand her own mind, led her at nineteen to establish her two schools. She yearned for knowledge of the world and longed to convey this knowledge to pupils, both rich and poor (poor, as she had been), the latter occupying a room over the stable. The pupils responded eagerly to her teaching, aware how avidly she wanted them to learn so they would have a more equitable chance in life.

She felt delighted when a few wealthy families sent their children from towns as far distant as Portsmouth, New Hampshire. At this time, Boston had a population of only forty thousand, but contributed its share of young students to Dorothea's more elegant schoolroom in Dix Mansion.

At age twenty-one, in 1823, Dorothea began a correspondence that would last the rest of her life with a young woman who became a close friend, Miss Anne Heath of Brookline, Massachusetts. One day in the church parlor on Federal Street, Mrs. Channing, the wife of Dorothea's beloved minister, walked over to Dorothea. She asked her to befriend a young girl who was so shy she always sat by herself in church.

From the moment they met, Dorothea and Anne felt at home with each other. Dorothea wrote of feelings she would never have confessed to anyone else. Luckily, many of their letters were preserved and quoted by Tiffany in his book.

Anne told Dorothea that she made all the clothes for her sisters, brothers, and cousins, with whom she lived in a large farmhouse in Brookline. According to Baker, Dorothea spoke of her engagement to Edward, confessing that she did not know why she feared marrying him.

She also informed Anne that she intended to devote her life to important, useful work. She referred to the poor children at the gate of Dix Mansion whose suffering had always moved her deeply. No doubt it reminded her of the suffering she had endured before her grandmother took her into Dix Mansion.

Anne saved Dorothea's many letters, some of which show the world her powerful desire to help the unfortunate, but at times describe her deep depression. She did not hesitate to convey this depression to Anne.

In Tiffany's words, "Self-repressed and self-mastered as later on she outwardly fronted the world, inwardly her soul was in those days full to the brim of passion and heart-break, of poetic enthusiasm and religious exaltation. Her demands on herself, her demands on her friends, her demands on her pupils, were out of all bounds. And so the inevitable reaction from such overwrought expectations was subjection to hours of bitter disillusion and even of passionate, unjust censure of average, commonplace mortality." Tiffany understood Dorothea well.

She wrote her new friend Anne in 1823 of the work of Letitia Elizabeth Landon, a young Englishwoman, referred to in the letter as "L. E. L."

> *Dear Annie,—You say I weep easily. I was early taught to sorrow, to shed tears, and now, when sudden joy lights up or any unexpected sorrow strikes my heart, I find it difficult to repress the full and swelling tide of feeling. Even now, though alone and with no very exciting cause of joy or grief, I am paying my watery tribute to the genius of L. E. L.*
>
> *Oh, Anne! she is a poetess that expresses all the genius and fire of Byron, unalloyed with his gross faults; all the beautiful flow of words which fall like music on the air from the pen of Moore, without his little less than half-concealed consciousness; all the simplicity of Wordsworth without his prosiness and stiffness; finally, in the words of her reviewer, "If she never excels what she already has written, we can confidently give her the assurance of what the possessor of such talents must earnestly covet, immortality." The "Improvisation" will soon be*

published in this country and then, Anne, prepare for the enjoyment of this rich feast.

I worship talents, almost I sinfully dare mourn that I possess them not. . . . It is not that I may win the world's applause that I would possess a mind above the common sphere, but that I might revel in the luxury of those mental visions that must hourly entrance a spirit that partakes less of earth than heaven. . . . I shall try to feel and to act better but I cannot cease to lament.

> *Good night,*
> *Thea.*

It is interesting that she signed her letter with the last four letters of her name, which she used only when she wrote to Anne. This signature was the part of her that expressed her poetic feelings. "Thea" is a far more ethereal name than "Dorothea."

But in the next five years, the strain of each day's work, exhausting in itself, slowly took a high toll on Dorothea's body. Dorothea rose before the sun and did not fall asleep until after midnight, reading, always reading, wanting to learn more of poets and philosophers. She also sought textbooks, such as the *Science of Common Things*. She had no leisure time (perhaps did not wish any, so she would not think of her earlier, unhappy life with her mother and father). There was little joy in the house because her grandmother fell gravely ill.

She explained in a letter to Anne: "Anne, my dear friend, if ever you are disposed to think your lot an unhappy one, or your heart desolate, think of her whose pathway is yet more thorny, and whose way is cheered by no close connections. You have an almost angelic mother, Anne; you cannot but be both good and happy while she hovers over you, ministering to your wants, and supplying all that the fondest affection can provide. Your sisters, too, they comfort you. I have none."

Dorothea bared her heart about her wish for a more loving mother. She most certainly did not possess an "angelic mother," but one who was ill most of her life and neglected her daughter and two sons. Dorothea did not receive "fondest affection" or "comfort." All she could say about her earliest life was, "I never knew childhood!"

Overworked, Dorothea grew thin and felt feverish. Dr. Channing, seeing her in church, warned, "A virtue carried to excess may also be a vice."

One day she crossed the yard at Dix Mansion and pulled open the heavy door downstairs before climbing the stairs of the carriage house for her session at the charity school, called "The Hope." Suddenly, she felt a warm bubbling in her throat. She coughed into her handkerchief and saw blood. She continued upstairs to teach the class.

A few weeks later, when she tried to rise in the morning, she fell back on the bed as blood once again gushed from her throat. She was taken to Massachusetts General Hospital, where Dr. H. S. Hayward, her doctor, announced that she had "rheumatism of the lungs." She was ordered to stop teaching and lay ill for several weeks at home as her grandmother sat by her bed.

Dr. Channing frankly counseled her in a letter:

> *I look forward to your future life not altogether without solicitude, but with a prevailing hope. Your infirm health seems to dim your prospects of usefulness. But I believe your constitution will yet be built up, if you will give it a fair chance. You must learn to give up your plans of usefulness, as much as those of gratification, to the will of God. We may make these the occasion of self-will, vanity, and pride as much as anything else. May not one of your chief dangers lie there?*
>
> *It is said that our faults and virtues are sometimes so strangely interwoven that we must spare the first for the sake of the last. If I thought so in your case, I would withhold my counsel, for your virtues are too precious to be put to hazard for such faults as I might detect.*

One outcome of her relationship with Dr. Channing, who obviously admired her, was an invitation to undertake the education of his two young daughters for six months during spring and summer 1827. Dr. Channing had a large country home in Portsmouth, Rhode Island, overlooking Narragansett Bay and invited Dorothea to stay with his family during those months. He assured her that her duties would be light; she could sit in the open air, which would help cure her illness.

He had another motive, too. During this period, he wanted her to teach his daughters in preparation for their starting school. He assured her she could help them even as she lay on the couch all day.

She accepted the invitation both to relax in the sun and to teach his daughters. She enjoyed the flowers, the seaweed, the shells, and the marine life. When the summer ended in early October, Dr. Channing wrote thanking her, adding, "I wish to say to you that if you should think another summer's residence on Rhode Island would be beneficial to you, Mrs. Channing and myself would be glad to again engage your services for our children. I dare not urge the arrangement, for I have an interest in it."

Over the next few winters, Dorothea's pulmonary weakness caused her to seek refuge from the severe winter climate of New England. She stayed in Philadelphia for a while, then Alexandria, Virginia, keeping herself busy reading poetry, science, and biographies. She started to write books, among them *Common Things, Conversations,* which was published by Munroe & Francis in Boston in 1824 (it reached its sixtieth edition in 1869); *Ten Short Stories for Children,* 1827–28; *Meditations for Private Hours,* Boston, 1828, with a number of subsequent editions; *The Garland of Flora,* Boston, S. G. Goodrich & Co., 1829; and *The Pearl, or Affection's Gift; a Christmas and New Year's Present,* Philadelphia, 1829.

Even though she still suffered physically, she refused to relax completely, always finding some way to keep up her spirits. One winter she wrote Anne:

> *Dear Annie,—I am never less disposed to sadness than when ill and alone. Sometimes I have fancied that it was the nature of my disease to create a rising, elastic state of mind, but be that as it will (I speak solemnly), the hour of bodily suffering is to me the hour of spiritual joy. It is then*

*that most I feel my dependence on God and his power to
sustain. It is then that I rejoice to feel that, though the
earthly frame decay, the soul shall never die. The discipline which has brought me to this has been long and
varied; it has led through a valley of tears, a life of woe. . . .
It is happiness to feel progression, and to feel that the
power that thus aids is not of earth.*

The following is an extract from another letter written during this
period:

*Last night, dear Annie, I could not sleep, and after several
restless hours rose at one o'clock, wrapped myself warmly
in my flannel gown, and was in search of my medicine,
when the remarkable clearness of the sky drew me to my
window. There was Orion with his glittering sword and
jeweled belt, Aldebaran, the fiery eye of Taurus, Saturn
with his resplendent train of attendants, and the sweet
Pleiades; there, too, flamed Canicula and Procyon, beneath whose rival fires the beautiful star of evening had
long since sunk from view; Leo with his glorious sickle
followed in the train, and thousands on thousands of
starry lamps lent their brightness to light up the vast
firmament that canopied the silent earth,—silent, for
sleep had exerted its restoring influence upon all save the
sick and sorrowing. I turned reluctantly again to seek my
weary couch. With feelings of gratitude to my God for all
his past goodness and humble trust in his future care, I
laid my head on my pillow, and though I could not sleep
could meditate.*

In autumn 1830, when she was twenty-eight, Dorothea was invited by Dr. Channing to accompany his household to a more exotic
place—the tropical island of St. Croix. Dr. Channing was seeking to
recuperate from impaired health. They sailed in the schooner *Rice
Plant* from Boston on November 20, 1830. St. Croix, often sought as
a refuge by consumptive patients, is twenty-three miles long and six
miles wide, from which the Blue Mountain rises to a height of eleven

hundred feet. Visitors feel that it is almost like being at sea when they stay there.

Dorothea delighted in a literal paradise of trailing vines, palms, bananas, rare birds, shells, and marine plants. As she wrote her friend, Mrs. Samuel Torrey:

> *Another letter from you, my dear friend, impels me to take up my pen. I think that this incitement would not have been needed had I been under any other influence than this before-named* languor. *Our darling Mary, the cook, says, "How changed Miss Dix is! She used always to be busy, and now she only says, 'Don't talk to me!' and throws herself on the bed twenty times a day."*
>
> *I am also the unfortunate subject of Dr. Channing's jests. "My dear," he says to Mrs. Channing, "Where can Miss Dix be? But I need not ask—doubtless very busy, as usual. Pray, what is that I see on yonder sofa, some object shrouded in white? Oh! that is Miss Dix, after all. Well, well, tell it not in Gath! How are the mighty fallen!" All this I hear, but I am rising above it in more than one sense. I am really getting well—or well over this vexatious* no-disease *that does nothing, thinks nothing, is nothing.*

While in St. Croix, in addition to an exhaustive study of all the physical features of the island, she read constantly, as always, and wrote full extracts from the saints and sages of all periods and all lands, including Hindu, Persian, Greek, and Christian sources.

In a later letter to Tiffany, one of Dr. Channing's daughters recollected Dorothea at this time, referring also to the summer she spent in Portsmouth:

> *She was tall and dignified, but stooped somewhat, was very shy in her manners, and colored extremely when addressed. This may surprise you who knew her only in later life, when she was completely self-possessed and reliant. She was strict and inflexible in her discipline, which we, her pupils, disliked extremely at the time, but for which I have been grateful as I have grown older and found how much I was indebted to that iron will from*

which it was hopeless to appeal, but which I suppose was not unreasonable, as I find my father expressing great satisfaction with her tuition of pupils. . . . Fixed as fate we considered her.

We all became much attached to her, and she was our dear and valued friend, and most welcome guest in all our homes. She was a very religious woman, without a particle of sectarianism or bigotry. At the little Union Meetinghouse which adjoined Oakland, our place on Rhode Island, Miss Dix always had the class of troublesome men and boys, who succumbed to her charm of manner and firm will. Later on, after the death of her grandmother, she was a constant visitor at our home. She delighted to drop in unexpectedly, and then suddenly receiving a letter from a poor soldier at Fort Adams, would start off at a moment's notice to right his wrong and persuade the government to improve the arrangements for the comfort of the men.

The long vacation in St. Croix restored her to health. She was ready to work in behalf of the children of Boston, to help them with spelling, arithmetic, composition, geography, and history. She had missed them and yearned to return to her "two schools" at Dix Mansion.

3

THE SWIFT VICTORY

Restored to almost normal health, Dorothea once again resumed teaching her two classes at her home. In fall 1831, when she was twenty-nine, she learned that General Levi Lincoln, whom she had met at her grand-aunt's home in Worcester, was elected the new governor of Massachusetts and that her second cousin, Edward Bangs, who had given up pursuing her, was appointed secretary of state to Governor Lincoln. She also was told that Edward had married Mary Grosvenor, born of a prestigious Boston family. The couple now lived in Boston near the capitol on Beacon Hill.

For the next five years, Dorothea worked as if driven by spirits and demons. She again rose before dawn and fell into bed after midnight. As her grandmother grew more and more feeble, Dorothea took care of her as best she could. She wrote Anne, "There is so much to do, I am broken on a wheel."

A number of her pupils at this time were interviewed by Tiffany when they were adults. They reported that although they had felt "overstimulated" at times, they were grateful for the knowledge they acquired in their personal contact with Dorothea.

One student wrote nearly sixty years later, "Dorothea fascinated me from the first, as she had done many of my class. Next to my mother, I thought her the most beautiful woman I had ever seen. She was in the prime of her years, tall and of dignified carriage, head finely shaped and set, with an abundance of soft, wavy, brown hair."

After five difficult years of teaching the two separate classes and caring for her grandmother, Dorothea broke down completely in spring 1836. Hemorrhages recurred; the old pain in her side seemed fixed, "as though a splintered lance were there," in Tiffany's words, "and her exhausted nerves would respond no further. She had achieved her cherished ends, though at a fearful cost. Her labors had secured for her the independence of a modest competence; she had made a home for, educated and helped embark in the world her younger brothers; she had won a position of dignity and respect as a teacher, and had set a stamp never to be effaced on a large number of young minds."

Tiffany added, "Only it looked as though she had been self-slain in the process."

The frequent hemorrhages caused her to feel exhausted all the time. In some of her letters, she referred to her "lung difficulty." Her illness was not then called "tuberculosis" (a term that became popular in the next century), but was given such names as "pulmonary weakness," "a condition of the lungs," "consumption," and "symptoms of lung congestion with tendency to hemorrhage." In Tiffany's words, "her lungs became inflamed."

After Dorothea lost the use of one lung, her doctors insisted she had to give up the idea of teaching and take a long vacation. Dr. Channing suggested that she go to England, where friends of his had taken care of him when he was ill of a similar sickness.

He provided her with a letter of introduction to Mr. and Mrs. William Rathbone of Liverpool, whom he described as his "saviors," and to other influential persons in London. Dorothea set sail from New York City to Liverpool on April 22, 1836, at the age of thirty-four, accompanied by Dr. and Mrs. Frank Schroder. The Schroders were friends of Dr. Channing, who said they would watch over her carefully during the voyage. Dorothea intended to spend several months in England recuperating and then explore the Continent.

When the ship docked at Liverpool, she went straight to the Liverpool Hotel and to bed, too ill to travel or sightsee. The Rathbones visited her at the hotel and insisted on taking her at once to their large home in Greenbank, three miles outside the city. Mr. Rathbone was a wealthy merchant, in high standing in the community, who also worked for many social reforms, Dr. Channing had informed her.

Dorothea planned to remain no longer than a few weeks at the Rathbones' comfortable house, but stayed eighteen months. She suffered frequent hemorrhages, feeling so exhausted that she could not leave her bed. Yet, to the end of her days, Tiffany reported, she considered these months the most relaxing of her life, "the sunniest, most restful and the tenderest to her affections of her whole earthly experience."

The Rathbones gave her a sense of loving care she had lacked her entire life. They made her feel wanted, something she had never known in childhood, when her parents were the needy ones, or in adulthood, with her emotionally detached grandmother. The long stay in Liverpool proved the only real holiday she ever took. In spite of her illness, or perhaps because of it, she seemed in a relaxed state of mind, not driven to *do* anything but sleep and recover her sense of well-being.

She wrote on October 1, 1836, to Mrs. Torrey in Boston:

You know I am ill. You must imagine me surrounded by every comfort, sustained by every tenderness that can cheer, blest in the continual kindness of the family in which Providence has placed me—I with no claims but those of our common nature. Here I am contracting continually a debt of gratitude which time will never see canceled. There is a treasury from which it will be repaid, but I do not dispense its stores. I write from my bed, leaning on pillows in a very Oriental luxury of position,—one I think will soon fall into a fixed habit.

Her grandmother wrote her that it seemed an "outright moral fall" that her own granddaughter would consent to remain month after month in a strange household where she paid nothing, luxuriating in her lazy life. Her grandmother did not understand how ill Dorothea was, how the loss of the use of one lung affected her both mentally and physically.

Dorothea replied, daring to be honest with her grandmother: "I have felt the obligation to my friends in England so exclusively my own that it was not less surprising than painful to know you indulged so much solicitude on that point. There is a danger, perhaps, of my getting a little spoiled by so much caressing and petting [which she never received from her grandmother], but I must try to do without it if I get better. So completely am I adopted into this circle of loving spirits that I sometimes forget I really am not to consider the bonds transient in their binding."

She then wrote Mrs. Torrey: "You know all my habits through life have been singularly removed from any condition of reliance on others, and the feeling, right or wrong, that *aloneness* is my proper position has prevailed since my early childhood, no doubt nourished and strengthened by many and quick-following bereavements."

She was about to experience another bereavement. She received a letter on September 28 from Mrs. H. S. Hayward of Boston, telling of the death of Dorothea's grandmother and a few days later, the death of Dorothea's mother. The two most important women in Dorothea's life had abandoned her forever at the same time. Even though she had seen little of her mother after she was twelve, Dorothea's childhood memories, as with all of us, would be permanent and strong. Mary Dix had received financial help from Madame Dix as long as she lived.

In her letter, Mrs. Hayward assured Dorothea: "The remembrance of duties so faithfully performed, and the consciousness that you could have done nothing more for your grandmother had you been at home, will be a comfort to you. Your mother's departure was so unexpected that even those in the room were totally unprepared; no sickness nor suffering but a sudden summons to go to her rest after a life of suffering from a lingering disease." We have no knowledge what that disease was; perhaps, like Dorothea, it was "disturbance of the lungs."

Dorothea's mixed feelings for her grandmother must have combined sorrow for the death of a woman who had taken her into her lavish home and allowed her to open schools there, with anger at a woman who was unable to express any sign of love and deep feelings for her granddaughter.

Nearly nine months after her arrival in England, on January 25, 1837, Dorothea wrote Anne that, for the first time, the doctor had given her permission to walk around the room several times daily, and it had been ten days "since the last spitting of blood."

Despite the two deaths in her family, Dorothea's health improved slowly. She wrote Anne that for the first time she had sat on the lawn, looking up at the Gothic mansion in which she had lain so ill and then at the River Mersey, flowing toward the slums of Liverpool. She had been told that each year fifty thousand slaves were shipped from Liverpool to America.

Mr. Rathbone took her to see the slums, telling her that he gave half his large income each year to the poor. He was descended from a family of shipowners who grew rich from their trade but donated funds to the impoverished, including Englishwomen with chains around their bodies, crawling on hands and knees to draw coal through the dark passages in the mines.

When Dorothea left the Rathbones in Liverpool to return home, Mr. Rathbone handed her a book he thought she would like to read. It was the British translation of the writings of Dr. Philippe Pinel of Paris, the first doctor to free the insane from their chains. Mr. Rathbone told Dorothea that Pinel was "the great liberator" of the mentally ill. She carried the book in her portmanteau on the voyage home in autumn 1837 and later read it carefully.

From Pinel, Dorothea learned that throughout the Middle Ages the mentally ill were beaten and tortured to "drive the devils out of their supposed victims," as it was put. They were chained, whipped, and bled to death when they showed violent outbreaks of fury. Up to 1770, Bethlehem Hospital in London, popularly known as "Old Bedlam," was full of madmen cursing, raving, and fighting like wild beasts. The less angry men and women were guarded by brutal keepers, ready at the slightest sign of rebellion to knock them senseless with heavy clubs.

In Paris, at the height of the French Revolution, when the wards

of asylums were filled with violent patients, Dr. Pinel, on receiving
the appointment of superintendent of Bicêtre, the asylum for incurably insane men in 1792, ordered, "Off with these chains! away with
these iron cages and brutal keepers! They make a hundred madmen
where they cure one. The insane man is not an inexplicable monster.
He is but one of ourselves . . . underneath his wildest paroxysms
there is a germ, at least, of rationality and of personal accountability.
To believe in this, to seek for it, stimulate it, build it up,—here lies
the only way of delivering him out of the fatal bondage in which he is
held!"

Pinel kept urging these humane convictions on the Commune and
eventually was allowed to treat the "madmen" more kindly. He
witnessed the recovery of several prisoners in less than a year. Over a
short period he released from their chains more than fifty "maniacs,"
including merchants, lawyers, priests, soldiers, and laborers.

In 1796, four years after Pinel's first experiment, a similar reform
was inaugurated in England, not by a physician, but by a member of
the Society of Friends, William Tuke, Mr. Rathbone's grandfather.
Tuke was a merchant of ample fortune and feelings of pity for the
insane. With his own money, he built The Retreat at York, where the
mentally ill were treated humanely. The Retreat became a landmark
in its caring attitude toward those who had temporarily lost their
minds or those who might never recover.

According to Tiffany, Pinel and Tuke "were the two original minds
that inaugurated a new epoch in the history of the treatment of
insanity, an epoch as revolutionary in character within this especial
realm as that of the Copernican system in the realm of astronomy. It
implied an absolute reversal of all previous conceptions; the substi-
tution, in the place of restraint and force, of the largest possible
degree of liberty; the abandonment of the whole previous idea of
brute subjection for that of the emancipation of the reason and the
enhancement of the sense of personal responsibility. Each one of
these remarkable men achieved his task uninformed of the action of
the other."

Dorothea also learned that at the start of the nineteenth century,
there were only four insane asylums in the United States, of which
only one had been built by a state government. The first was opened
in Philadelphia in 1752; the second, the first state asylum, in Wil-

liamsburg, Virginia, in 1773; the third, in New York in 1791; and the fourth, in Baltimore in 1797. In 1817 a number of Philadelphia Friends collected funds and opened a hospital in which the insane were "regarded as *men* and *brethren.*" One year later the McLean Asylum in Belmont, just west of Boston, opened; in 1824, The Retreat in Hartford, Connecticut, was founded; and in 1830, the State Hospital in Worcester, Massachusetts was started. These hospitals applied the new scientific and humane ideas inaugurated by Pinel and Tuke.

Before she left England, Dorothea did not explore the Continent, as she thought she might; after an absence of eighteen months, she decided to sail back to Boston. She thanked the Rathbones with all her heart for helping to heal her, feeling vastly improved and returned in autumn 1837 to an empty Dix Mansion, her grandmother gone forever and her brothers living elsewhere.

Through her grandmother's will, she received a bequest that, along with the earnings of her days of teaching, provided money for her moderate wants during the rest of her life. As Tiffany summed it up, "she was thus made mistress of her own time."

Not intending to teach again, Dorothea wandered for the last time through the empty rooms and closed the big house on Orange Court. While she was in England, there occurred a third important death: that of her second cousin, Edward, who once proposed marriage to her.

Doctors in Boston advised her not to spend the winter in the severe New England climate. Her grandmother's will permitted her to live wherever she chose for the rest of her life. That winter of 1838 she spent a short while in Washington, D.C., then went to Oakland, near Alexandria, Virginia. But she felt unhappy; in England she had the sense of being loved and wanted, taken care of in an atmosphere of sympathy. As she wrote Anne from Washington on February 24, 1838:

> *I was not conscious that so great a trial was to meet my return from England, till the whole force of the contrast was laid before me. Then, I confess, it made an impression which will be ineffaceable. . . . Perhaps it is in myself the fault chiefly lies. I may be too sensitive; I may hunger and*

*thirst too eagerly for that cordial, real regard which exists
not in mere outward forms or uttered sounds; I may be too
craving of that rich gift, the power of sharing other minds.
I have drunk deeply, long, and oh! how blissfully, at this
fountain in a foreign clime. Hearts met hearts, minds
joined with minds; and what were the secondary trials of
pain to the enfeebled, suffering body when daily was administered the soul's medicine and food. Yes, beloved, ever
too dearly beloved ones, we are divided, and what but the
deepness of sorrow, what but the weight of grief, would
rest on my soul, if the Future, the glorious Future, the
existence that knows no death, no pain nor separation,
were not seen in the long vista through which Faith and
Hope are the angelic conductors!*

*But there are duties to be performed here. Life is not to
be expended in vain regrets. No day, no hour, comes but
brings in its train work to be performed for some useful
end,—the suffering to be comforted, the wandering led
home, the sinner reclaimed. Oh! how can any fold the
hands to rest, and say to the spirit, "Take thine ease, for all
is well"!*

These words proved prophetic. Before long her compassionate
heart and dauntless wish would be "brought face to face with an
abyss of human misery in the condition of the helpless and outcast
insane throughout the land, so appalling in the scenes it opened up
that from that day forward till extreme old age left Dorothea helpless, she would never want for activity," as Tiffany put it.

Dorothea mourned a fourth death of someone she loved when Dr.
Channing died in October 1841. Dr. Channing had often spoken of
"man's inhumanity to the stricken poor." He had instilled in her the
awareness that even in the most degraded persons there could be a
mental development if they were treated humanely. As soon as she
became interested in the pitiable condition of the poor insane, it was
not mere sentimental compassion over their sufferings that occupied
her mind but the question, "What class of positive forces, philanthropic, medical, legislative, judiciary, can be summoned into the
field to cope with this awful problem?" Tiffany reported.

Her friend Horace Mann was well aware of the miserable status of the mentally ill. He objected, as Dorothea did, to the federal law of 1816 that made it the duty of the United States Supreme Court "to commit to prison any person whom a grand jury refused to indict or a jury to convict by reason of his mental condition, and to keep him confined there until his health came to be compatible with his release and the public safety, or until a friend would assume responsibility." The law would not be changed until 1827 when "persons furiously mad" were committed to the "state hospitals" (originally called lunatic asylums) instead of to the former jails and almshouses.

Occasionally Dorothea would recall how she had started out by inspecting the living conditions of every insane person in the state of Massachusetts. She had wanted to make a personal survey; she would not accept anyone else's word. She took notes on every jail, farmhouse, or poorhouse where the "pauper insane" were chained. She began what she considered this vital survey the day she left Dr. Channing's house at 85 Mount Vernon Street, backed by his approval of what she intended to do. It took her eighteen months before she could report to him the misery she had discovered.

She now started to look at the whole question of insanity—its origin, its stages of development, its relation to body and mind, its treatment, and the legal and moral rights of the insane—as well as to acquire knowledge of the most advanced thoughts on what today we call mental health.

She was about to become the apostle of a new wave of caring that would kindle the humane and scientific enthusiasm not only of the nation's leaders in the few hospitals already established to help the wealthy insane, but of leaders of the future who would dedicate their lives to the poverty stricken mentally ill. She haunted libraries, read further about the treatment of the insane in this country, who had no Pinel to rescue them. She learned of the McLean Asylum, just west of Boston, and The Retreat in Hartford that accepted for treatment only those men and women who could pay for it.

She would shortly find herself pleading a cause of which at this moment in her life she was unaware, though it had slowly been unfolding in her mind. The yearnings she felt for the completion of her new goal would be far more intense than those that had led to her establishment of schools for young pupils.

In winter 1841, Dorothea decided, in spite of her doctors' orders, to return to Boston when snow was still on the ground. It was on March 28, following the Sunday sermon at church, that she heard the two men walking behind her talk about the horrors in the East Cambridge Jail, of the insane poor penned in dark caverns.

She had become aware, through Mr. Rathbone's philosophy and Dr. Pinel's book, that, as Tiffany described it, "the terrible superstitions of the Middle Ages, which had always sought the explanation of insanity in the idea of diabolic possession, and had seen in its frenzies of imprecation, filthiness and blasphemy simply the masterpiece of Satan, still hung like a lurid cloud over the human mind. . . . The real king who was finally to dethrone these imaginary supernatural terrors had not yet seated himself on the throne." In the case of America, the "king" would be a woman.

Why was it a woman? At this period in history, middle- and upperclass women as a rule were not permitted to work in occupations or spheres considered the province of men. There were no women in state legislatures or in Congress, women did not even have the right to vote. Why did Dorothea dare enter this territory and why was she accepted so swiftly by the men in power?

There are no doubt many reasons Dorothea's compassion and quiet intensity appealed to the male legislators. These men sensed at once her high intelligence and her dedication to what they either consciously or unconsciously knew was a valid, important issue neglected for centuries—the humane care of the mentally disturbed. Many of these men had children and relatives who suffered and they understood the need to help the indigent insane.

They also were moved by her deep desire to take care of the less fortunate, realized all her energy was devoted to this task. Massachusetts had been a leader in providing a hospital for wealthy disturbed men and women, why should it not lead in the provision of care for the poor?

These men also became aware of a strength in Dorothea that had led to her consuming desire. Her father's love, as much as he could give, emotionally disturbed himself, was beneficial, as was her grandfather's obvious love. Dorothea's relation to him, even though he died when she was seven, gave her courage later to face a world controlled by men.

Dorothea felt comfortable enough within herself to dare act as few women had, up to this time in history. She was not afraid to go it alone, as was proved in her eighty-five years. She was independent, but part of her appealed deeply to men who admired her wish to help the unfortunate, cut off from daily life because of inner traumas.

At the age of thirty-three, she had to give up, as Tiffany described it, "a life devout and heroic in purpose, and a life marred by willful overstrain. A hectic fever had long been running in her blood, which raised to a perilous intensity the self-sacrificing impulses and the moral and religious ardor of her temperament. She had as yet learned no law of limit." Her life, he added, "was like seeking to dwarf into the hull of a little launch a marine engine powerful enough to drive an ocean steamship, in the teeth of the roughest gales, across the Atlantic."

Dorothea also conveyed to the men at the top Dr. Channing's insistence on the presence in human nature, even in the poor insane, of recovery from illness of the mind. She was convinced that philanthropic medical, legislative, and judiciary forces should join to cope with what she thought was inhumanity to man, perpetuated by man.

As Tiffany put it, she discovered that "a madhouse was a menagerie, nothing more." She wanted to rescue from this sordid stereotype those who could not speak for themselves.

She had first visited the East Cambridge Jail in 1841, fifteen years before Sigmund Freud was born on May 6, 1856. Freud did not express his famous psychoanalytic theories on the treatment of the emotionally ill, including those who had lost their sanity, until the 1890s.

After visiting other Massachusetts jailhouses, where the poor barely existed, and receiving the help of leading Bostonians in championing her cause, Dorothea must have felt elated. She, a woman, had earned the respect of men. This first victory no doubt inspired her to continue, to seek to help other states nearby and then throughout the land. She had to feel an accomplishment far beyond any she had yet achieved. It was a vastly different, far more rewarding enterprise than teaching school. A large part of what she would accomplish was to teach mankind the value of helping those who could not help themselves.

In her work over the years until she died, Dorothea alone would be responsible for setting into motion a vast program that would, at long last, provide the indigent, mentally disturbed men and women with livable quarters, decent food, and the chance, under knowledgeable psychiatrists and nurses, to regain their sanity.

The conclusion of her *Memorial* before the Massachusetts State Legislature contained an impassioned appeal for adequate provision against the continuance of such horrifying quarters for the insane:

> *Men of Massachusetts, I beg. I implore. I demand pity and protection for these of my suffering, outraged sex. Fathers, husbands, brothers, I would supplicate you for this boon—but what do I say? I dishonor you, divest you at once of Christianity and humanity, does this appeal imply distrust? . . . Here you will put away the cold, calculating spirit of selfishness and self-seeking, lay off the armor of local strife and political opposition; here and now, for once, forgetful of the earthly and perishable, come up to these halls and consecrate them with one heart and one mind to works of righteousness and just judgment. . . . Gentlemen, I commit to you this sacred cause. Your action upon this subject will affect the present and future condition of hundreds and thousands. In the legislation, as in all things, may you exercise that wisdom which is the breath of the power of God. Respectfully submitted.*
> *D. L. Dix.*
>
> *85 Mt. Vernon Street, Boston*
> *January, 1843.*

Her *Memorial* exploded like a bombshell, according to Tiffany. It was a graphic indictment not of a local evil here and there, but of an evil that prevailed more or less in every township throughout the Commonwealth of Massachusetts—probably every state of the union.

Dorothea had now acquired on her side a number of prominent men, including Dr. Howe, Dr. Channing, Horace Mann, the Reverend John G. Palfrey, and Dr. Luther V. Bell of the McLean Asylum. These men represented a tower of psychic strength.

She possessed what Tiffany called "a statesmanlike grasp of mind," as well as a "sensitive heart." She now received praiseworthy letters from her supporters. Dr. Bell, known for his humanity and sound practical judgment wrote: "I pray that you may have a reward higher than the applause of the world."

Horace Mann in his letter said, "I have felt in reading your *Memorial*, as I used to feel when formerly I endeavored to do something for the welfare of the same class,—as though all personal enjoyments were criminal until they were relieved."

Dr. Channing, who had written an eloquent description of her *Memorial* for the *Christian World*, wrote her, "I only wish it were more worthy. Such as it is, I give it to you with my best thanks for your great work of humanity." Lucius Manlius Sargent, a highly respected Bostonian, warned her, "I trust you will not suffer a moment's disquietude from the consideration that there is a morbid sensibility abroad which may question the propriety of such an investigation by one of your sex."

Shortly after its first presentation to the Massachusetts Legislature, the *Memorial* was referred to a committee of which Dr. Howe had been appointed chairman. The committee made a report at once, strongly endorsing Dorothea's plea and fortifying it with other instances of similar outrages against humanity.

The report closed with an eloquent appeal for immediate action by the legislature, after pointing out that the entire provision of care for the insane in the state was directed at wealthy patients in the state hospital at Worcester and the McLean Asylum, whereas there were in the commonwealth at least 958 pauper, insane and "idiotic" persons receiving no care.

Committee Chairman Dr. Howe, an important backer of Dorothea's plan, had been eager for her bill to pass. He remained by her

side all the way, encouraging her every effort. As the debate proceeded, he sent her short, stimulating letters.

In one letter he announced:

> *I presented your* Memorial *this morning, indorsing [sic]
> it both as a memorial and a petition. Your work is nobly
> done, but not yet ended. I want you to select some news-
> paper as your cannon, from which you will discharge
> often red-hot shots into the very hearts of the people, so
> that, kindling, they shall warm up the clams and oysters of
> the house to deeds of charity. When I look back upon the
> time when you stood hesitating and doubting upon the
> brink of the enterprise you have so bravely and nobly
> accomplished, I cannot but be impressed with the lesson
> of courage and hope which you have taught even to the
> strongest men. . . . You are pleased to overrate the impor-
> tance of my efforts. I can only reply that if I touch off the
> piece, it will be you who* furnish the *ammunition.*

So profound was the sensation throughout the commonwealth
awakened by the hideous details and impassioned eloquence of
Dorothea's *Memorial* that the instructions and delays of the politicians were swept away before a steadily rising tide of public indignation. A bill for immediate relief was carried by a large majority. An
order was passed to provide state accommodations at the Worcester
state hospital for two hundred additional insane persons.

The Reverend Palfrey, congratulating Dorothea, wrote that Dr.
Howe "managed the business admirably—like the man of humanity,
energy, and abundant resources, as he is."

This was Dorothea's first legislative victory, the start of many more
to follow throughout the country and eventually in other countries.
The victories would add up eventually to a magnitude that as-
tounded everyone, including Dorothea.

Her friends, of which she had many, always admired the quality of
her voice, which Tiffany described as "sweet, rich and low, perfect in
enunciation," adding, "its every tone pervaded with blended love
and power." He described her as "quiet but always tasteful in the
style of her dress, her rich, wavy, dark brown hair brought down

over the cheek and carried back behind the ears, her face lit with alternately soft and brilliant blue grey eyes."

Possibly Dorothea felt two opposing feelings at her first success. She had to feel elated in the support of the important men in the legislature. She had to know she had champions in men who would help her further what by now had become her life's mission, one she believed extremely important. Then she might have spontaneously thought of the frustration at what lay ahead, perhaps saying to herself, "I have been successful, but now I really have to face the immense need for help. I feel both happiness and sadness—not depression but sadness—at the thought of the suffering of the hundreds of thousands of the poor who are mentally disturbed and need to be understood, not treated like wounded animals. It's like ploughing; you break the ground and see a huge, endless field in front of you."

But she knew she would not stop, could not stop, having started the climb upward. Once she saw her desire could be fulfilled, there were no excuses for her to withdraw.

At this point she recalled how the doctor told her she might have only a year to live, what with one lung useless, and Dr. Channing saying, "Then make that year do."

Could a woman with only one lung accomplish what was almost a miracle? It would depend on the inner strength of the woman, "that iron will from which it was hopeless to appeal," in Dr. Channing's words.

Dorothea was a shy woman, as she had been a shy little girl. But she was also a determined woman, as she had been a determined little girl. Like her father, she preferred handing out words on paper, rather than speaking them. She never addressed a group, spoke only to individuals about her cause.

It was not easy to travel through the country in those days, as some of her letters attest. Carriages broke down, drivers were irresponsible, passengers were held up by thieves. Yet she preferred these hazards to a safe life, as she waged her fight in behalf of the mentally ill.

Traveling, for her, became part of a mission whose hard work kept her from feeling lonely. In a few letters to Anne she confessed her loneliness but then always included enthusiastic words about her work. Travel, in one way, became her savior. At that time it proved an adventure to go by horse and carriage throughout the country. Dorothea must have been reminded of the delightful times when she and her beloved grandfather explored Boston in his carriage.

Her future was determined, she realized, as she became aware that all over the country, from Maine to Florida, from the Atlantic to the Mississippi, the insane poor were subject to the same appalling conditions and treatment. Everywhere they were "thrown into cages, closets, cellars, stalls, pens and chained, beaten with rods and lashed into obedience," as she wrote in her first *Memorial*.

She now thought that if one legislature could understand and pass a bill to help the indigent insane, why could not the legislatures of every state? She decided she had nothing but time and would, state by state, accumulate the facts, prepare her written "communication" in the form of a *Memorial*, then contact the various legislatures to ask the support of their leaders.

It would be a vast campaign, but she had the hours for thorough research. This work could not be half as wearying as teaching school. She could spend all the time she needed to study the proper treatment for the indigent insane. Her first act was to consult Dr. John S. Butler, superintendent of the newly erected Lunatic Hospital of Boston in 1839. Six years before, when starting the practice of medicine in Worcester, he had met Dr. Woodward, who helped the rich insane in his hospital. Dr. Butler had seen what he thought miraculous triumphs in the restoration to sanity of violent, mad souls. He was now ready to help the poor understand their illness.

He wrote an article on "Insanity" for the *North American Review* in 1842 in which he said of his new hospital:

> *Its patients are wholly of the pauper class. Its inmates are of the worst and most hopeless class of cases. They are the raving madman and the blithering idiot, who, in the language of the inspectors of prisons, hospitals, etc., for Suffolk County, we had formerly seen tearing their clothes amid cold, lacerating their bodies, contracting most filthy habits, without self-control, unable to restrain the worst feelings, endeavoring to injure those that approached them, giving vent to their irritation in the most passion-*

ate, profane, and filthy language, fearing and feared, hating and almost hated.

Now they are all neatly clad by day, and comfortably lodged in separate rooms by night. They walk quietly, with self-respect, along their spacious and airy halls, or sit in listening groups around the daily paper, or dig in the garden, or handle edged tools, or stroll around the neighborhood with kind and careful attendants. They attend daily and reverently upon religious exercises, and make glad music with their united voices.

Dorothea became Dr. Butler's pupil, learning what progress, slow though it might be, could be made if the "raging madhouse of the past" became "the humane retreat of the present," in Tiffany's words. He called this "a transformation which is unquestionably the most marvelous triumph ever won by the moral reason of man over brute chaos."

She wrote Anne from Lexington, Kentucky, on December 22, 1843:

I left Boston in September, as you know, visited en route the prisons on Long Island and in the city of New York, also went to those of New Jersey, and duly reached Philadelphia. There and at Harrisburg I was detained a fortnight. Proceeding to Baltimore, I visited prisons there, and so on as far as Pittsburg west. Thence to Cincinnati, where I arrived the last of October.

The first of November I came to Kentucky, and have been laboriously traveling through the counties, collecting facts and information ever since, except a week which I took in Tennessee. The Legislature being in session in Nashville, I desired to do something for the state prison. This effected, I crossed the country by a rapid journey to Louisville, traveling by stage two days and nights. I proceed to-morrow to the northeast counties, if well enough. I have engaged lodgings in Frankfort, Ky., for January and February, and shall probably go to the Southern prisons after the Legislature rises in this State.

Dorothea relied on the men who would vote for a new mental hospital, ignoring the few who thought it was more important to spend the money to educate the children of the state. Although any new building was still "a castle in the air," she visualized the ample and beautiful grounds; the stately new structure; the quiet, home-like wards; and the wise and tender care of those who would look after the insane, friendless, and wretched of that state.

She did not know it then, but the day was drawing near when, in twenty different states, as Tiffany put it, "she was to see with the bodily eye such an outward and tangible witness of the power of her own inner life as is rarely given to a mortal to behold."

Dorothea wrote Mrs. Hare in Philadelphia from aboard a steamboat on the Ohio River, "I have had some of the most delightful evidences of good accomplishing the past week. I am very happy, and wonder, while such holy rewards reach me for effort and sacrifice, if I should ever find myself faltering, or sighing for the life of repose, which, in the distance, seems to me so attractive."

She would never enjoy that "life of repose" until she lost the ability to walk, but not to think, thirty-nine years later. Tiffany wrote that at this earlier time in her life, "Look on this picture and on this!" had become "more than the Hamlet cry" of Dorothea's heart.

4
DOROTHEA'S "FIRSTBORN" CHILD

After conducting her special investigations into how cruelly the poverty-stricken insane were treated in her home state, Dorothea crossed the border into other states. In the first state she visited, Rhode Island, she saw the same misery. She spoke to legislators there, including Thomas G Hazard, a prominent leader, who offered to help her.

Hazard wrote to the Rhode Island newspapers about Dorothea's work, saying, "In the course of her investigations she has ferreted out some cases of human suffering almost beyond conception or belief,—one case in a neighboring town to this, of which I was yesterday an eyewitness, which went beyond anything I supposed to exist in the civilized world, and which, without exaggeration, I believe was seldom equalled in the dark ages."

The case to which he referred centered on a man, Abram Simmons, confined in a dungeon in Little Compton. Dorothea later wrote of it in an article entitled "Astonishing Tenacity of Life," which was published in the *Providence Journal* on April 10, 1844. She did not use her name because she always preferred to keep herself in the background. She referred in this instance to the testimony of Mr. Hazard before the legislature.

She described the cell of Abram Simmons:

> *His prison was from six to eight feet square, built entirely of stone and entered through two iron doors, excluding both light and fresh air, and entirely without accommodation of any description for warming and ventilating. The internal surface of the walls was covered with a thick frost, adhering to the stone in some places to the thickness of half an inch. The only bed was a small sacking stuffed with straw. The bed itself was wet, and the outside covering was completely saturated with the drippings from the walls and stiffly frozen.*
>
> *Thus, in utter darkness, encased on every side by walls of frost, his garments constantly more or less wet, with only wet straw to lie upon, and a sheet of ice for his covering, has this most dreadfully abused man existed through the past inclement winter. His teeth must have been worn out by constant and violent chattering for such a length of time, night and day.*

She had been warned not to enter his cell because he was known as a man of fury who would surely attack and kill her. But, she wrote, after entering the "horrible den, there he stood, near the door, motionless and silent; his tangled hair fell about his shoulders; his bare feet pressed the filthy, wet stone floor; he was emaciated to a shadow, etiolated, and more resembled a disinterred corpse than any living creature."

She went on:

> *Never have I looked upon an object so pitiable, so woestruck, so imaging despair. I took his hands and endeavored to warm them by gentle friction. I spoke to him of release, of liberty, of care and kindness. Notwithstanding the assertions that he would kill me, I persevered. A tear stole over his hollow cheek, but no words answered*

my importunities, no other movement indicated con-
sciousness of perception or sensibility.

In moving a little forward I struck against something
which returned a sharp metallic sound; it was a length of
ox-chain, connected to an iron ring which encircled a leg
of the insane man. At one extremity it was joined to what
is termed a solid chain,—namely, bars of iron eighteen
inches or two feet long, linked together, and at one end
connected by a staple to the rock overhead.

When she asked the prison guard how long Simmons had been kept in the prison, he told her "about three years . . . he was kept in a cage first; but once he broke his chains and the bars and escaped; so we had this built, where he can't get off."

Dorothea wrote in a comment, "No, indeed; as well might the buried dead break through the sealed gate of the tomb!"

While in Rhode Island she met Cyrus Butler, a businessman who ultimately left an estate of four million dollars but, as she said, "who, like so many men absorbed in the pursuit of wealth, had contracted a passion for accumulation that rendered it well-nigh impossible to persuade him to give a dollar away." She was determined nonetheless to call on him even when a number of people advised her it would be like "getting milk out of a stone."

She was accompanied to his home by the Reverend Edward B. Hall of Providence, who left her at the door to fend for herself. At first, Mr. Butler tried to shift the conversation to the familiar topic of the weather. Finally Dorothea said quietly, "Mr. Butler, I wish you to hear what I have to say. I want to bring before you certain facts, involving terrible suffering to your fellow-creatures all around you, suffering you can relieve. My duty will end when I have done this, and with you will then rest all further responsibility."

She told him, in her soft, persuasive voice, what she had seen with her own eyes of the treatment of the insane poor. He listened "spellbound," according to Tiffany, then said abruptly, "Miss Dix, what do you want me to do?"

She said in her soft, appealing voice, "Sir, I ask you for $40,000 toward the enlargement of the insane hospital in this city."

He stared at her, then said, "Madam, I'll do it!"

Tiffany wrote, "Probably there was not another woman in the land who could have commanded such combined power of cogent statement and impassioned fervor as thus, in an hour, to reverse all the deeply rooted habits of a lifetime. The feat attracted great attention at the time in Providence. Miss Dix always spoke of Mr. Butler with sincere respect, and felt most gratefully his service to the cause she had so close at heart."

The name of the asylum was changed to Butler Hospital in honor of his generosity. In later years, further large endowments were given by Alexander Duncan, who married Mr. Butler's niece, heiress to his fortune.

This was Dorothea's second victory. In two states she had been able to transfer several hundred of the poor insane from dangerous dungeons and inhumane treatment to what were later called mental hospitals. She was starting to awaken in the legislators and in the public the need to help restore to sanity the most unfortunate group in the nation.

Comparatively few of the states as yet had any asylums, for the rich or for the poor. Dorothea now became even more determined to enlarge the scope of her work. She also wanted to change the pattern of care from one of "supplementing" the deficiencies of already existing institutions to "creating" new institutions, progressive in their thoughts about restoring mental health to both the poor and the wealthy.

She decided to tackle a third state. She headed for New Jersey, specifically Trenton, the capital. There, as Tiffany reported, "she went through the travail of bearing beneath her heart what she ever after characterized as her 'first-born' child, owing its whole life to her as the mother."

This "child" would, forty-five years later, supply her with a home when, worn out with toil, age, and disease, she would die in a special apartment on the top floor, named after her. This space had been held for her free use over the years by the trustees.

To describe in detail all the public institutions that she founded single-handed would take volumes. She originally started by going unobtrusively and alone to take notes of the condition of a jail where the indigent insane were prisoners. Nothing escaped her now well-trained eyes as she gathered statistics.

The preliminary work finished, she would resort to personal influence among influential people in the political and social worlds. She appeared as a quiet but determined leader. Dr. P. Bryce, superintendent of the asylum at Tuscaloosa, Alabama, once described her as "truly marvelous," saying he had "never met anyone, man or woman, who bore more distinctly the mark of intellectuality."

Perhaps more important, she was careful not to make enemies. She believed enmity to her brought enmity to those she sought to help.

When it came to the art of engineering a bill through a legislature, she insisted on placing full responsibility into the hands of the political leaders. Her *Memorial* once written, she would then decide who to ask to back it in the legislature.

Dr. Eugene Grissom, superintendent of the insane asylum at Raleigh, North Carolina, described how Dorothea worked quietly behind the scenes. He reported:

> *The first appropriation bill looking to the erection of an asylum in North Carolina was defeated. Mrs. Dobbin, wife of Hon. James C. Dobbin, of Fayetteville, afterwards Secretary of the Navy, was very sick at Raleigh. Her husband was a member of the House. On her death-bed she expressed to Miss Dix her deep gratitude for the tender care that noble woman had given her in her illness, and, almost with her dying breath, begged her gifted husband to repay her own debt of gratitude to Miss Dix by another effort to pass the asylum bill.*
>
> *Almost as soon as the last sad services of interment were ended, Mr. Dobbin entered the House, clad in the deepest mourning and broken with sorrow. He entered at once on the fulfillment of the duty he owed to the pious dead and the afflicted living. Feeling keenly his own bereavement and cherishing sympathy for the woes of others, he redeemed nobly his last promise to a dying wife by a speech which made a great impression at the time, and the*

tradition of which has descended to this generation. . . .
All opposition disappeared under the power of the elo-
quent and pathetic pleader and the bill passed by an over-
whelming vote.

Dorothea made such a profound impression in her ability to carry
the state legislatures that when she appeared, a special room in the
library was set apart for her, in which members could visit her. She
studied in advance the list of the representatives in the assembly,
trying to learn which ones were interested in the humane approach
rather than just servile to public opinion. She did not enter the halls
of legislation or seek interviews with the members in their homes or
in the lobbies. Members of both houses were brought to her by
influential friends, either in the alcove or in her own room. She
sometimes invited into the parlor of her temporary boardinghouse
from fifteen to twenty gentlemen at a time to plead her cause in her
always pleasurable voice. After her *Memorial* was read to the legislature, then brought to the general public through the newspapers,
she wrote articles trying to rouse strong public opinion all over the
state.

Her vitally important *Memorial* to the legislature of New Jersey
was presented to the Senate on January 23, 1845, by her staunch
supporter, the Honorable Joseph S. Dodd. As with all her other
public papers, it combined strong rational arguments with a deep
appeal for the insane poor. She wrote of those she had first seen in
Massachusetts:

> *One whom I was so fortunate as to have removed to a*
> *situation of greater comfort, and to supply with some of*
> *the common necessaries of common life, said, raising his*
> *trembling arms reverently, "God's spirit bids this message*
> *to you, saying it is His work you are doing; lo, it shall*
> *prosper in your hands!" Another, a female, whose scarred*
> *limbs bore marks of the cankering iron worn for many*
> *weary years, said, "I could curse those who chain me like*
> *a brute beast, and I do, too, but sometimes the* soft *voice*
> *says, Pray for thine enemy, and this it sings often while*
> *the sun shines on the poor mind; but darkness comes, and*

then the thoughts are evil continually, and the soul is black!"

The Senate and General Assembly of New Jersey voted to adopt Dorothea's plan on February 25, 1845. They announced that the *Memorial* "presents the whole subject in so lucid a manner as to supersede the necessity of further remarks from us."

Dorothea wrote her friend Mrs. Hare of Philadelphia:

> *I must write to you, I must have your sympathy. How I long for your heart-charming smile! Just now I need calmness; I am exhausted under this perpetual effort and exercise of fortitude. At Trenton, thus far, all is prosperous, but you cannot imagine the labor of conversing convincingly. Some evenings I had at once twenty gentlemen for three hours' steady conversation. The last evening, a rough country member, who had announced in the House that the "wants of the insane in New Jersey were all humbug," and who came to overwhelm me with his arguments, after listening an hour and a half with wonderful patience to my details and to principles of treatment, suddenly moved into the middle of the parlor, and thus delivered himself: "Ma'am, I bid you good-night! I do not want, for my part, to hear anything more; the others can stay if they want. I am convinced; you've conquered me out and out; I shall vote for the hospital. If you'll come to the House and talk there as you've done here, no man that isn't a brute can withstand you; and so, when a man's convinced, that's enough. The Lord bless you!" and thereupon he departed.*

There were those who objected, such as the senator who said, "Let us husband our resources. I had rather spend the money in educating the children of the State . . . qualifying them to act their part well in life, and preparing them for eternity." He added contemptuously, "I should like the whys and wherefores for a building 487 feet long and 80 feet wide, for, maybe, twenty lunatics."

Dorothea spent a portion of the years 1843 to 1845 in New Jersey, either collecting statistics from county to county or working with members of a legislature that moved slowly. Often the legislature was not in session or engaged in other matters.

She also set out to tackle the neighboring state of Pennsylvania. Entering the capital, Harrisburg, she worked hard in what proved to be another successful campaign. The date of the passage of her bill for founding a new state institution in Pennsylvania corresponded closely with the passage of the bill in New Jersey.

Buoyed by her success, she embarked on long and arduous journeys from Nova Scotia in Canada to New Orleans. She visited Ohio, Kentucky, Indiana, Arkansas, Illinois, Missouri, Georgia, and Alabama. Dr. Howe wrote from Boston on July, 1845:

> *As for you, my friend, what shall I say to you to express my feelings respecting your course since I have seen you personally? Nothing, for words would fail me; besides you want not words of human praise.*
>
> *I look back to the time when the whisperings of maiden delicacy made you hesitate about obeying the stern voice of conscience. I recollect what you were then, I think of your noble career since, and I say, God grant me to look back upon some three years of my life with a part of the self-approval you must feel! I ask no higher fortune. No one need say to you, Go on! for you have heard a higher than any human voice, and you will follow whither it calleth. God give you as much strength as you have courage, for your mission!*

Dorothea wrote Anne: "At Sea. Steamer Charleston, from Savannah to Charleston.—a Storm, Lying to.

> *A temporary quiet induces me to use the only writing materials I have now at hand. I designed using the spring and summer chiefly in examining the jails and poorhouses of Indiana and Illinois. Having successfully completed my mission to Kentucky, I learned that traveling in the States referred to would be difficult, if not impossible, for some weeks to come, on account of mud and rains. This decided me to go down the Mississippi to examine the prisons and hospitals of New Orleans, and, returning,*

to see the state prisons of Louisiana at Baton Rouge, of Mississippi at Jackson, of Arkansas at Little Rock, of Missouri at Jefferson City, and of Illinois at Alton.

I have seen incomparably more to approve than to censure in New Orleans. I took the resolution, being so far on the way, of seeing the State institutions of Georgia and South Carolina. Though this has proved excessively fatiguing, I rejoice that I have carried out the purpose.

Fatigue as well as peril was involved in journeying these thousands of miles in 1845, as compared to the speed, ease, and luxury with which the same distances are reached today. Nothing then existed of the large networks of railways (much less airlines) that enabled riders to cover swiftly every nook and cranny of the United States.

There were the steamboats on the rivers and a few lines of coaches and private conveyances that could be hired on land. What Tiffany called "the craziest of vehicles, the most deplorable roads, and taverns whose regulation diet of corn bread and 'bacon and greens' would have undermined the digestion of an ostrich," were the rule, not the exception, in the South and West.

From chilly autumn rains to the warmth of the following spring, the endless stretches of the clay lands of the South and West turned into seemingly bottomless mud. The drivers of the coaches were usually Negroes or "poor whites." Malarial fever could strike at any moment, the lack of medicine and medical skill ensuring its rapid spread.

Dorothea remained undaunted, a lone and unprotected woman, as she headed for every quarter where abuse was present or an almshouse awaited inspection. Of the large number of *Memorials* she would write and present to the country's legislatures, each was a different, moving account describing the primitive, cruel treatment of the insane poor.

Tiffany describes Dorothea as "one more illustration of the so common saying that the work of the world is done by its invalids." He compared this result to the question of "why an engine of ten horsepower, its piston-rod packed tight and its valves fitting with precision, was capable of as much work as an engine of twenty horse-power, its draught choked with soot and its cylinders leaking steam at every joint." He added, "careful invalids, consecrated to arms, science, or humanity, manage to wrest from the wreck of their lungs, nerves or digestion" as much working force as strong giants.

Dorothea maintained her deep interest in nature's beauty. Even though she would suffer hemorrhages or become prostrate with malarial fever again and again, her brain remained active. Throughout her life, she never spoke of a headache. When she felt weary, she would take to bed and sleep thirteen to sixteen hours to tide her over the next few nights of riding in uncomfortable vehicles on bumpy roads. There seems little doubt that some people can overcome physical illness by mental thoughts. In Dorothea's case, she was so driven and so successful with her cause that it dominated her physical disability as she saw arising before her one new hospital after another to house the poverty-stricken mentally ill. At the end she would found outright or vastly change thirty-two mental hospitals in this country.

Every so often she wrote Anne, always maintaining what Tiffany called her "invincible reticence" to talk about herself. In one letter she reported she had encountered "nothing so dangerous as river fords. I crossed the Yadkin where it was three fourths of a mile wide, rough bottom, often in places rapid currents; the water always up to the bed of the carriage, and sometimes flowing in. The horses rested twice on sand-bars. A few miles beyond the river, having just crossed a deep branch two hundred yards wide, the axletree of the carriage broke, and away rolled one of the back wheels."

She sent Anne an item written by a reporter that appeared in the Greenville, South Carolina, *Patriot*. Entitled "An Interesting Incident," it described "a remarkable incident" in Dorothea's travels:

> The other day, in conversation with Miss Dix, the philanthropist, during her visit to Greenville, a lady said to her, "Are you not afraid to travel all over the country alone, and have you not encountered dangers and been in perilous situations?"
>
> "I am naturally timid," said Miss Dix, "and diffident like all my sex; but in order to carry out my purposes, I

*know that it is necessary to make sacrifices and encounter
dangers. It is true, I have been, in my travels through the
different States, in perilous situations. I will mention one
which occurred in the State of Michigan.*

*"I had hired a carriage and driver to convey me some
distance through an uninhabited portion of the country. . . . In pursuing our journey through a dismal-looking
forest, a man rushed into the road, caught the horse by the
bridle and demanded my purse. I said to him, with as
much self-possession as I could command, 'Are you not
ashamed to rob a woman? I have but little money and that
I want to defray my expenses in visiting prisons and poorhouses, and occasionally in giving to objects of charity. If
you have been unfortunate, are in distress and in want of
money, I will give you some.'*

*"While thus speaking to him I discovered his counte-
nance changing, and he became deathly pale. 'My God,'
he exclaimed, 'that voice!' and immediately told me that
he had been in the Philadelphia penitentiary and had
heard me lecturing to some of the prisoners in the adjoin-
ing cell, and that he now recognized my voice. He then
desired me to pass on, and expressed deep sorrow at the
outrage he had committed. But I drew out my purse and
said to him, 'I will give you something to support you
until you can get into honest employment.' He declined, at
first, to take anything until I insisted on his doing so, for
fear he might be tempted to rob some one else before he
could get into honest employment."*

The results Dorothea had accomplished by the end of 1845
seemed miraculous. Four years before, in March 1841, the Reverend John T. G. Nichols had expressed serious fears of Dorothea's
survival because of her feeble health when she took over his Sunday
school class in East Cambridge Jail.

Now she was writing Mrs. Rathbone in Liverpool: "I have traveled
ten thousand miles in three years. Have visited eighteen State peni-
tentiaries, three hundred county jails and houses of correction, more
than five hundred almshouses and other institutions. I have been so

happy as to promote and secure the establishment of six hospitals for the insane, several county poorhouses and several jails on a reformed plan."

The six insane asylums to which she referred were the Worcester, Massachusetts, Asylum, greatly enlarged; the Butler Asylum (later called the Butler Hospital) in Providence, Rhode Island, practically refounded; the Trenton and the Harrisburg asylums, her own creations, and the Utica, New York, asylum, which had doubled in size. To these was added the sixth, in Toronto, Canada West. Of her work in procuring the reformation of jails and almshouses, Horace Mann called it "as wonderful a record as her more special work in behalf of the insane."

The following years saw Dorothea conducting a series of campaigns that called for her deepest resources. Her *Memorials*, different each time, carried the legislatures of Indiana, Illinois, Kentucky, Tennessee, Missouri, Mississippi, Louisiana, Alabama, South Carolina, North Carolina, and Maryland. She also established two new asylums in the British provinces, one at Halifax, Nova Scotia, the other at Saint John, Newfoundland.

During these active years, many of her letters to friends told of her growing success in the field she felt to be her life's work. She wrote Mrs. Hare from Raleigh, North Carolina, on November 27, 1846:

> They say, "Nothing can be done here!" I reply, "I know no such word in the vocabulary I adopt!".... This morning after breakfast several gentlemen called, all Whigs, talked of the hospital, and said the most discouraging things possible. I sent for the leading Democrats; went to my room and brought my Memorial, written under the exhaustion of ten weeks' most fatiguing journeys and labors. "Gentlemen," I said, "here is the document I have prepared for your assembly. I desire you, sir, to present it," handing it to a Democrat popular with his party, "and you, gentlemen," I said, turning to the astonished delega-

*tion, "you, I expect, will sustain the motion this gentle-
man will make to print the same."*

*They took leave, I do sincerely think, fully believing in a
failure, but I thought I could not have canvassed the State
for nothing. So the result proved. The Memorial was presented; the motion to print twelve extra copies for each
member was offered and passed without one dissenting
vote. These steps are then safely and successfully made.*

Dorothea received many public votes of thanks from legislators
and letters of congratulations of the type Dr. R. S. Steuart of Baltimore wrote after the passage of her bill in Maryland: "Most cor-
dially do I congratulate you on *your* success, because I am well
convinced that no other means than yours could have produced this
result. I am glad you have one more leaf added to the chaplet that so
honorably adorns your brow."

Letters from governors, legislators, and physicians' associations
poured in from all parts of the Union. Tiffany asserts, "On no other
page of the annals of purely merciful reform can be read such a series
of moral triumphs over apathy, ignorance, and cruel neglect as were
in that space of time won by Miss Dix."

He visualized the summoning before the mind's eyes of "the
buildings, farms, pleasure-grounds, skilled and humane supervision
of a great institution, taking into its protecting arms of mercy such
numbers of the most wretched and abandoned of earth's creatures."

She received a letter from Dr. Francis Lieber, of Columbia, South
Carolina, entitled, "Te Deum Laudamus!" which asked, "Who do
you feel like? Like a general after a victory? Oh, no! much better.
Like people after a shipwreck? You are saving thousands, and not by
one act, but by planting institutions, and institutions of love. And
when man does that, he comes nearest to his God of love and mercy.
Deus tibi lux!"

Another letter from Dr. Lieber, written November 5, 1846, from
Columbia, South Carolina, expressed the doctor's sense of the
unique moral and imaginative position occupied by Dorothea in the
work to which she had dedicated her life. He told her: "You as a
woman have a great advantage over us, for with the firmness, courage and strength of a male mind you unite the advantage of a

woman. . . . You do not excite the opposition; no one can suspect you of ambitious party views, and you can dare more because people do not dare to refuse you many a thing they would not feel ashamed of refusing to any one of our sex. Therefore take care of yourself!"

Dr. Lieber's admiration was mirrored also in his letter to Dr. George S. Hillard of Boston, in which he wrote: "Miss Dix is greatly exhausted, and I always fear to hear that she has succumbed somewhere in a lonely place. What a heroine she is! May God protect her! Over the whole breadth and length of the land are her footsteps, and where she steps flowers of the richest odor of humanity are sprouting and blooming, as on an angel's path. I have the highest veneration for her heart and will and head."

What was the secret of Dorothea's power? Writing in 1891, Tiffany pointed out that in her ideas "lay the hiding-place of the peculiar power she exerted in the Southern and Southwestern States, then ruled by an ideal of womanhood which had in it many elements handed down from the days of chivalry."

She believed strongly in a woman keeping aloof from anything savoring of ordinary political action and from every desire of material reward, whether money, place, or personal distinction. Woman had to be "the incarnation of a purely disinterested idea appealing to universal humanity, irrespective of party or sect." Woman was both a voice of tender supplication for the outcasts of the Earth and their impassioned champion, capable of flaming "with sacred fire," in Tiffany's words.

She once said she shrank with a distinct "moral repulsion" from certain politicians with whom she was brought into close contact, calling them "the meanest and lowest party demagogues . . . the basest characters."

By nature, she was, as one admiring friend said, "aristocratic in every fibre," learning this quality from her grandmother, grandfather, and father, mentally ill though her father might have been at times. Dr. Lieber also bestowed on her the name "anthophila," meaning the flower lover in Greek. This name held true not merely of her love of flowers, but of everything characterized by social grace and refinement, intellectual distinction or "beauty of manners, spirit and character," as Tiffany termed it.

The only belief that enabled Dorothea to tolerate contact with jailers who mistreated the insane, as well as with public characters who appeared offensive, was an unending compassion for human misery. She also had a fiery indignation at the infliction of mental pain and a lasting abhorrence of the brute, irrational chaos of a society that permitted such evils to exist.

Southern newspapers spoke of the arrival within their borders of that "gracious lady," that "crown of human nature," that "chosen daughter of the Republic," and that "angel of mercy." Dorothea was careful not to antagonize anyone over the "slavery question," which aroused hotly agitated discussions that awoke fierce hatred in the hearts of Northerners. She kept silent, knowing that if she spoke as a Northerner, she would jeopardize all chances of success in her own work.

She had exulted in her firstborn child as the legislators at Trenton voted to build a new institution for the needy insane. Dr. H. A. Buttolph became the superintendent of the mental hospital that Dorothea would always cherish as special—the first she created from the ground up. She was now on her way to producing many more such "children," her prime goal for the rest of her life.

5

THE TONIC OF OPPOSITION

Dorothea now received two additional tasks She discovered that after a state legislature passed a bill to pay for an asylum for the pauperized mentally ill, she was asked to shoulder the responsibility of selecting a site. She also had to decide the structure of the new building. Her choices, she soon realized, were as valid as those of anyone else.

She kept in touch with the few experts who, as superintendents of mental hospitals for the wealthy, slowly evolved plans that, over a period of years, would make American insane asylums the models of the civilized world.

As early as 1845, when Dorothea, at the age of forty-three, secured the founding of a hospital at Harrisburg, Pennsylvania, James Lesley wrote that she could rest assured "your wishes on the subject of site and buildings will be law. . . . No man nor woman other than yourself, from Maine to Louisiana, could have passed the bill under the discouraging circumstances with which you had to contend."

Dorothea now realized she had to ask the legislatures for more money to support the many asylums that were being created in response to her pleas. Each asylum cost $50,000 to $200,000 to build and furnish. She was prepared to play for even higher stakes—not in the halls of state legislative assemblies but in the arena of the U.S. Senate and the House of Representatives.

In 1848 she asked Congress for a grant of five million acres of the public domain, proceeds of the sale to be set aside as a perpetual fund for the care of the indigent insane. The sum total of this fund would be divided among the thirty states of the Union in proportion to their respective populations. Dorothea's first attempt to obtain this grant failed. At a subsequent session of Congress she raised the amount of her plea to 12,225,000 acres.

Dorothea believed that obtaining this fund would be the crowning glory of her life. A steady income, growing in volume with the increase of the population throughout the nation, would be secured in perpetuity for the poverty-stricken men, women, and children who temporarily lived in mental black pits of hell.

The original thirteen colonies along the Atlantic Ocean that had gained independence and were now states claimed a share of the vast areas of unoccupied lands lying to the west, which they had individually ceded to the federal government. Through purchase and conquest over the years, this area had grown to vast proportions. As new territories were formed into states and admitted to the Union, the same claims were accorded them.

With a public treasury overflowing with revenue from the sales of land in the public domain to settlers, representatives in Congress thought it wise to distribute such a surplus to the states every now and then. The new states almost exclusively received immense tracts of land. In 1845 an aggregate of 134,704,982 acres were granted to develop a system of general education and internal improvement. More than a billion acres of public domain still remained unassigned, however.

The disposition of public lands from the start had been wise, especially because it provided the foundation of school systems in the newly formed and thinly populated states to the west. But then private speculators, internal-improvement companies, and promoters of new lines of railway had taken over. Congress was besieged with demands for grants of land on a lavish scale.

The awareness of such greed inspired Dorothea with the thought of competing, seeking even more help for the needy indigent insane. She was aware this would be a risky, formidable undertaking, but was determined to give it a try.

She submitted her first *Memorial* to Congress on June 27, 1848, starting her campaign in the Senate. The *Memorial* was listed as Senate Bill 130131. By then, she had made friends among leading representatives of various states in which her name had become a household word. The *Memorial* was referred to a select committee, and five thousand copies were printed for use by the Senate.

In her *Memorial* Dorothea focused in a single appeal the story of her investigations throughout the country:

> *Present hospital provision relieves (if we do not include those institutions not considered remedial) less than three thousand seven hundred patients. Where are the remainder, and in what condition? More than eighteen thousand are unsuitably placed in private dwellings, in jails, in poorhouses and other often most wretched habitations.*
>
> *I have myself seen more than the nine thousand idiots, epileptics, and insane in these United States, destitute of appropriate care and protection; and of this vast and miserable company, sought out in jails, in poorhouses, and in private dwellings, there have been hundreds,—nay, rather thousands—bound with galling chains, bowed beneath fetters and heavy iron balls attached to drag chains, lacerated with ropes, scourged with rods, and terrified beneath storms of profane execrations and cruel blows; now subject to gibes and scorn and torturing tricks, now abandoned to the most loathsome necessities, or subject to the vilest and most outrageous violations. These are strong terms, but language fails to convey the astonishing truths. I proceed to verify this assertion, commencing with the State of Maine.*

Dorothea wrote Mrs. Hare, her Philadelphia friend, that her *Memorial*, while it "embodies facts," was open to severe criticism as a literary effort. She said she thought if Congress did not adjourn, she would pass on the bills, one asking for 5 million acres of the public surveyed lands for curable and incurable indigent insane, the other for 2 million acres for the blind, the deaf, and the mute. She added that she felt confidence only when an act was passed and signed by a governor or the president.

A new movement by the Democratic party in the northern states was threatening the free disposition of the land in the public domain. Those billion acres of public land still had not been sold, but it was now argued that the vast areas should be held for the prospective benefits of the poor—to sell the land now was robbery of the poor to enrich the powerful. The land sold at $1.25 or $1.50 an acre.

Dorothea realized that she sat between two fires. The opposition of the eastern states would frighten many Democratic politicians who did not want to incur the public's wrath by voting away another acre. And the material interests of syndicates of land speculators would drive them to fight against the intrusion of any new measure that threatened to swell the amount of public grants they wished to confine to their private channels.

Congress courteously assigned a special alcove in the Capitol Library to Dorothea. She sat there daily to talk to members of Congress in her quiet voice. To many of her friends, in and out of Congress, it appeared that her bill would pass both houses and receive the signature of President James K. Polk.

Dr. Luther V. Bell of the McLean Asylum in Somerville, Massachusetts, wrote on December 29, 1848:

> *Your friends cannot but trust that these terribly severe labors may be nearly at a close. And so, released by the actual accomplishment or encouraging inception of your labors, how much more remains to be done, which no one but you can do! The aggregation of misery and misfortune, of which you have sounded the depths, and have done so much to alleviate, affords yet an almost boundless field of labor with the pen, if possible of more moment than any present relief through personal devotion. In a country rushing upon the crowded population, the crimes, the miseries of the Old World with gigantic strides*

cannot something be done which shall tell *to all future time, by informing the world, at least the wise and good of the world, how these monster evils can be grappled with?"*

He suggested she take a year "and sit down to the composition of a volume which should meet the emergency alluded to. . . . A personal narrative of your last ten years of life would contain just the needful elements, if the fair conclusions could emanate from it, which you alone could do."

But first she had to await the congressional session of 1848–'49. She wrote her brother Joseph on January 30, 1849, that she thought the bill would be deferred until the next session. She explained that a new difficulty had arisen: President Polk had told his cabinet he would veto every land bill that did not make a provisional payment to the general public. She described herself as "neither sanguine nor discouraged."

The autumn and winter of 1849 found Dorothea in Montgomery, Alabama, trying to carry the state legislature. For two sessions the bill failed to pass, but during the third, in 1852, it did. One appropriation of $100,000 was secured, followed by another of $150,000.

Dorothea wrote Anne from Mississippi, "Twenty-four majority in the Senate, and eighty-one in the House, was something of a conquest over prejudice and the positive declaration and determination not to give a dime! Therefore, to give $250,000, besides the farm and foundations of the structure, is no small matter. Great was my surprise at the really beautiful vote of thanks, first by the legislature, then by the commissioners here and finally by the citizens. Legislature, commissioners and citizens alike insisted on naming the hospital after me." But she refused to allow them to do so, as she had on other occasions, because she did not permit any tribute in her name.

In this letter to Anne she also mentioned the hazards to which travelers on riverboats were exposed:

We have on our boat both cholera and malignant scarlet fever. To add to our various incidents, a quantity of gunpowder was left in charge of a raw sailor, who was directed, at a given time and place, to load the cannon and fire a salute. One hundred miles away from the point to be

> *so honored, Pat, the Irishman, thinking the bore of the cannon as good a place of deposit for the powder as he could find, rammed it down.*
>
> *Then discovering that the rain had wet the bore, he ran with alacrity to the furnace and returned with a burning stick, thrusting it in after the power, "to dry up the wather." This was effected; but not this alone, for of course the powder exploded, and certain portions of Pat's arm and hand were sent in advance toward the distant city.*

She did not mention it, but she undoubtedly took care of the unfortunate Pat, dressing his wounds. Dr. William G. Eliot, of Saint Louis, wrote her that she had an unerring instinct with which, on boarding a train or steamboat, she was sure, by a kind of freemasonry, "to detect any case of illness, poverty, or bereavement, and before long to be found ministering to it."

Many of the rich all over the country fought the establishment of asylums for the poor in their towns or counties. They did not want to live near "madhouses." Dorothea discovered this prejudice first in Maryland when wealthy landowners made it clear. Her supporter, the Honorable Thomas Donaldson, wrote from Annapolis: "There seems to be a soul of goodness in things evil, and you have reason to thank the malice of your opponents for the substantial aid which they give to the cause you advocate. The attack, coming from a masked battery, has raised you up friends that before were opponents, and has added the impulse of indignation to the cool conviction of your friends. The hospital never was so strong in the Legislature of Maryland. The letter of Teackle Wallis, printed in the Appendix of the Report, is really admirable, and it tells with great effect here. Every sentence cuts as cleverly and as cleanly as the Saladin's sword."

Her bill was deferred several times, finally allowed to lapse. But she did not give up hope. To her, this was only the first movement in an important campaign.

At the start of the congressional session of 1850, Dorothea asked Congress for the second time to vote in behalf of the indigent insane and the blind, deaf, and mute people of the country. The "tonic of opposition" had acted with its usual invigorating effect upon her, and she now proposed a higher bill—over twice as much—for 12,225,000 acres, of which 10 million would benefit the insane and 2,225,000, the blind, deaf, and mute.

This time the speedy success of her report was predicted by the press and enlightened public sentiment. At the annual conference of the Medical Superintendents of American Institutions for the Insane, a vote was passed unanimously, stating that the association "regards with deep interest the progress of the magnificent project which has been, and continues to be, urged by Miss D. L. Dix on the consideration of Congress, proposing the grant of a portion of the public domain by the federal government, the proceeds of which are to be devoted to the endowment of the public charities throughout the country, which meets with our unqualified sanction."

Once again Dorothea assumed her place in the alcove of the Capitol Library. Her day started at four or five in the morning. On rising, she set apart the first hour for religious devotions. After breakfast at eight, she went through her now overwhelming correspondence from asylums in twenty states. Ten o'clock saw her seated in her chair at the Capitol Library.

She was now forty-eight. Her soft brown hair showed scarcely a line of white, according to Tiffany, and "her blue gray eyes, so large and dilating in the pupils as often to be mistaken for black, retained all their range of expression from lightning-swift decision to tender compassion."

She studied language, as Tiffany put it, "as the soldier grinds his sword, to make it cut." She "studied the art of cogent statement and vital appeal as few orators study it. Few ever recognized more clearly the power of a fit word than she . . . her vocabulary became full, exact and varied."

As her friends by now expected, Dorothea rarely spoke of her own achievements. But she did so in a letter in June 1850 to Mrs. Rathbone: "Shall I not say to you, dear friend, that my uniform success and influence are evidence to my mind that I am called by Providence to the vocation to which life, talents, and fortune have been surrendered these many years? I cannot say, 'Behold, now, this great Babylon which I have builded!' but 'Lo! O Lord, the work which Thou gavest thy servant; she does it, and God in his benignity blesses and advances the cause by the instrument. He has fitted for the labor.' "

Summer 1850 was torrid in Washington, D.C., but Dorothea remained there and kept up hope. Her bill had passed the House of Representatives by a full majority. Deliberation in the Senate lay ahead. She wrote a friend on August 29, 1850: "None can tell what a mountain will be lifted from my breast if my bills pass. I shall feel almost as if I could say, 'Lord, let now thy servant depart in peace, for mine eyes have seen thy salvation!' . . . I ought to be ready to meet all changes, all events, but the troubles of the miserable world would, if now no way were opened for their alleviation, make the hour of death mournful to me."

The winter session of 1851 held delays in getting the bill called up in the Senate. Then Dorothea wrote Anne on February 11, 1851: "My dear Friend,—The bill has passed the Senate beautifully. A large majority, more than two to one!—thirty-six yeas to sixteen nays."

Before the bill could become an act, it had to pass both houses in the same session, then be signed by the president. For whatever their reasons, the House and Senate delayed joint action for nearly two years. During this time, Dorothea traveled in the southern, middle, and western states, encouraging them to start hospitals for indigent mental patients.

Congress voted an appropriation for founding an asylum for the insane of the army and navy in 1852. The domain selected for the asylum belonged to Thomas Blagden, who opposed it being built on his property. He wanted to keep the land for his family. Dr. John H. Nichols, who had worked hard toward the passage of the bill, made up his mind that he wanted that particular site. Congress had appropriated $25,000 but Mr. Blagden insisted he would accept no less than $40,000.

After exhausting every personal effort, Dr. Nichols, feeling depressed, sought out Dorothea. He said sadly, "There is nothing more to be done. We shall have to give the matter up, though it is the finest site in the world for a hospital."

She suggested in her quiet voice, "We must try what can be done." She went to see Mr. Blagden and pleaded so earnestly with him to help the thousands of his suffering fellow-creatures that he relented. He agreed to turn over the land for the amount Congress had appropriated.

When Dr. Nichols called on him to sign the requisite papers, Mr. Blagden complained, "I don't want to part with it," referring to his land. "It is dear to me and dear to my family. But I won't break my word to Miss Dix,—I won't break my word. I told her she should have it, and she shall have it!"

Mr. Blagden wrote her on the day she visited him, November 13, 1852: "Dear Madam,—Since seeing you to-day, I have had no other opinion (and Mrs. B. also) than that I must not stand between you and the beloved farm, regarding you, as I do, as the instrument in the hands of God to secure this very spot for the unfortunates whose best earthly friend you are, and believing sincerely that the Almighty's blessing will not rest on, nor abide with, those who may place obstacles in your way." He ended with the words, "With Mrs. Blagden's and my own most friendly regards, Very respectfully, Your obedient servant, Thomas Blagden."

Out of her pioneer work now emerged another important issue. Who should be the superintendents, assistant physicians, stewards, attendants, and nurses of the new asylums? The success of the historic undertaking depended on the capacities of those chosen to help the thousands of men and women who had lost their minds. A large number of doctors would soon turn in a new direction as they concentrated on helping those within the asylums try to regain their sanity.

Mrs. Louisa J. Hall, widow of the Reverend Edward B. Hall of Providence, Rhode Island, wrote a moving letter to Tiffany in 1889 after the sudden death of her husband. Tiffany had written, asking for her recollections of Dorothea. Mrs. Hall wrote that she met Dorothea in 1844 when her husband brought Dorothea to the house while she was campaigning for an asylum in that state.

Mrs. Hall stated that before she saw Dorothea, she had decided in advance that she did not like a woman who was a "self-appointed critic," but after meeting her and getting "one look at that calm, gentle face," she "began to feel the *gift* she had."

She continued, speaking of herself, "This foolish, obstinate conservative was conquered by the force of that beautiful, strong nature, shining through a genuine womanhood. . . . She stayed some

days with us, never introducing the subject, but ready to give information, and tell us of facts that made us bless the day she was born,
and the day when she found what work the Lord had for her."

Mrs. Hall presented this picture of Dorothea at that time: "She
traveled all over the country with a moderate valise in her hand, and
wearing a plain gray traveling dress with snow-white collar and cuffs.
Her trunk was sent a week ahead with the necessary changes of
linen, etc., and one plain black silk dress for special occasions.
Neatness in everything indicated her well-directed mind. And my
acquaintance with her helped me on the upward way from extreme
conservatism."

Another description of Dorothea was given by Dr. Isaac Ray of the
Providence mental hospital: "To have Miss Dix suddenly arrive at
your asylum and find anything neglected or amiss, was considerably
worse than an earthquake. Not that she said anything on the spot,
but one felt something ominous suspended in the very air."

Dorothea at times seemed to give the impression of possessing
many distinct personalities, as Tiffany points out. Some who met her
when she was silent and uncommunicative thought her self-centered
and unsocial. Others who felt her soothing touch called her "a
ministering angel." Many were aware of her organizing ability that
ended in victory as she triumphed over obstacles that would have
caused others to give up at once. She was hailed as a modern Joan of
Arc, fighting to create hospitals that would help return to normal
those who had lost their minds and had no money to pay for help.

Mrs. S. C. P. Miller of Princeton, New Jersey, wrote a memorial
tribute for the *Home Journal* of New York, printed September 11,
1889, two years after Dorothea's death. She recalled:

> *I saw her only when she was strong and self-collected, and
> believed that to be her normal condition. But there came a
> day when I got a new insight into her nature. I was in
> Richmond, and she, on a mission farther South, halted
> there and sent a note for me to come and see her. I went to
> the hotel immediately, was ushered into her room, and
> there found such a Miss Dix as I had never dreamed of.*
>
> *Overstrain of mind and body, destroying her calm exte-
> rior and bearing away the support of her high purpose,*

*had left her stretched upon a sofa, utterly weak, nervous,
and tearful. Not a bit of the heroism was left; only the tired
woman of a type I knew full well. Amazed at her condition,
I bent over her with a tenderness before unknown, and a
new bond of sympathy was established between us; so
strange is it, yet so true, that tears bring all women to the
same level.*

But even when Dorothea sank to a low point of physical prostration, she wrote a friend, "I shall be well enough when I get to Kentucky or Alabama. The tonic I need is the tonic of opposition. That always sets me on my feet."

Dorothea now undertook a different kind of mission for a short while. In June 1853, still awaiting the success or failure of her bill, at the age of fifty-one she was busy arranging for the foundation of a hospital in Saint John, Newfoundland. Suddenly, a violent storm in nearby Sable Island caused a number of severe shipwrecks, and many men and women drowned.

Dorothea, who had endured a few perilous experiences of her own at sea, decided to take action for the future rescue of those who faced such furious gales. She decided to visit Sable Island, named "The Graveyard of Ships." Sable Island jutted into the Atlantic, thirty miles south of the easterly end of Nova Scotia. She found it a "waste of desolate, windswept sand hills, fringed with everlasting surf, harborless and shelterless on every side," in Tiffany's words.

She wrote Anne:

*The whole region for leagues around is a trap and a snare.
One sunken bar stretches sixteen miles away to the northeast, another twenty-eight miles to the northwest. The
embrace of these long arms is death, for between them lie
alternate deeps and shoals, and when the sea is angry it
thunders and reverberates along a front of thirty miles,
extending twenty-eight miles to seaward.*

*No lighthouse throws its warning gleam beyond this
seething death-line, for stone structures will not stand
upon these ever shifting sands, and wooden ones of sufficient height could not withstand the storms. The mariner
drifts to his grave through total gloom. The whole island
bristles with stark timbers and the debris of wrecks. Thus
like the monster polypus of ancient story, it lieth in the
very track of commerce, stretching out its huge tentacles
for its prey, enveloped in fogs and mists, and scarcely
distinguishable from the gray surf that unceasingly lashes
its shores.*

Official records set the number of known wrecks on the island
between 1830 and 1848 at sixteen full-rigged ships, fourteen brigs,
and thirteen schooners. There was also the loss of a large number of
unknown vessels, engulfed and identified only by a floating spar.
Sable Island in 1598 had become a penal colony for convicts from the
French settlements in Arcadia, forty of whom had been deposited
there by the Marquis de la Roche and left to their fate. Seven years
later, only twelve had survived. An increasing commerce added to
the tale of wrecks; the island was sought by desperate "piratical
wreckers," according to Tiffany, who "gave it such a name that it was
reputed better for mariners to be swallowed up by the sea than to
escape only to be murdered on land."

Finally, in 1802, the year Dorothea was born, after the wreck of
the British transport, *Princess Amelia*, when the two hundred re-
cruits, officers, and servants all perished, some murdered by pirates,
the provincial legislature took action. A relief station was established, the wreckers were driven off the island and a superintendent, with a crew of four men, was placed in charge.

Tiffany questioned why Dorothea, in the days when women's
work was limited chiefly to the home, should become interested in
Sable Island. He asked why "an overtaxed and suffering representative" of the woman's sex "should see it in the light of imperative duty
to make a voyage to this so dreaded island, to study on the spot
whether something more effective could not be devised for the
safety of those exposed to such frightful perils."

He further asked, "Why her imperative duty? Were there not the home government and the provincial government; were there not admirals and captains in plenty; were there not the rich shipping merchants of Halifax, Liverpool, New York and Boston, whose argosies lay stranded at every point of those storm-lashed shores? And she herself? Surely with hospitals to look after in twenty States, 12,225,000 Acre Bills to engineer through Congress, and two new asylums actually in hand in Nova Scotia and Newfoundland, might she not guiltlessly have washed her hands of Sable Island?"

He concluded, "No, thither must she go, to study the problem on the spot, to examine into every detail of the life-saving apparatus used, and to leave behind her, as she scoured every part of the island on one of the ragged little wild ponies that breed there, 'the character of an intrepid horseman.' "

Even landing on Sable Island was dangerous, but Dorothea decided she must go and see the island for herself. There was no harbor, even on the north, the more sheltered shore. The vessels had to lie off at a considerable distance, ready at the first sign of an unfavorable wind to put out to sea.

Luckily for Dorothea, her visit occurred at a quiet time at sea. But a dense fog arose and, according to Tiffany, "she found herself within the fatal arms of the sand polypus" as the small boat in which she rode foundered. But all lives were saved. The scene was described by E. Merriam, of New York, who later carried out Dorothea's plan to equip the island with proper lifeboats and appliances:

> *The ship was abandoned by all but the captain, who had become a raving maniac and would not leave. Miss Dix rode to the beach on horseback, as the last boat landed from the ill-fated ship, and learned the sad fate of the commander, who, the sailors said, was a kind-hearted man.*
>
> *She plead with them to return to the wreck and bring him on shore, and to bind him if it was necessary for his safety. They obeyed her summons, and soon were again on the beach, with their captain bound hand and foot. She loosened the cords, took him by the arm and led him to a boathouse built for the shipwrecked, and there by kind words calmed his mind and persuaded him to thank the*

sailors for saving his life; she trusted that rest and
nourishing would restore him to his reason.

When Dorothea returned to the United States, she set to work on
her plans for Sable Island. She had discovered that the boats and the
lifesaving apparatus were far inferior to the requirements of the day.
The boats were clumsy and unsafe in view of the perilous services
demanded of them. There was no mortar for throwing a line across a
wrecked vessel and no provision of breeches buoys.

With her usual success, appealing at once to her friends among the
merchants of Boston, New York, and Philadelphia, she was provided
with funds for building boats of more modern construction. Two
months after her trip to Sable Island, on August 20, 1853, Dorothea
sought out experts in nautical matters, including Captain Robert B.
Forbes, chairman of the Humane Society of Boston, who quickly
responded to her appeal. Captain Forbes had founded the Sailors'
Snug Harbor for disabled seamen in Quincy, Massachusetts, and
the idea of saving lives on Sable Island appealed to his sense of
humanity.

Dorothea wrote him after arriving in Boston and asked to meet
him so that his "superior judgment and assistance can assist Miss
Dix's own aims." They met, and in his journal Captain Forbes wrote
on September 16: "Trying experiments with life-preservers and
boat, I went into the river with a neighbor to show Miss Dix how to
capsize and how to right a boat. We invited her to throw herself over,
and permit us to save her, but, as she had no change of clothes, she
declined."

In mid-November he wrote Dorothea, addressing her as "My
Dear Lady": "Your several notes are received. The last bears date,
Buffalo, 12th inst., and, as far as I can make out (you do write a hard
hand for a business woman), asks for an answer to New Jersey and
Trenton. Here it is."

Referring to one new boat, he told her it was being fitted with "her
floats" in Boston and he was "putting in copper air-tight cases. All
will, I trust, be ready for shipment in four or five days." He said he
had made a long journey to Williamsburg, "where your New York
boats are lying in the shop of Francis. They are good boats, though

rather heavy, and I predict that the 'Victoria' will be the queen of the fleet." He signed the letter, "I am very truly yours, R. B. Forbes."

Incidentally, his reference to her handwriting was also noted by all her correspondents, according to Tiffany, "who were often driven to their wit's ends in vain attempts to decipher it. The trouble began back in her school-keeping days, when overstrain added writer's cramp to her numerous disabilities. Things grew worse in this respect when so vast a correspondence was thrust upon her by her asylum work. Indeed, her biography could hardly have been written without an amount of serious preliminary study of her manuscripts, fairly equal to that of Champollion in his preparation for deciphering the hieroglyphics of Egypt."

The brig *Eleanora*, destined to carry the New York boats, sailed to Sable Island November 27, 1853. Unfortunately, the brig was driven ashore in bad weather and became a total wreck, as one boat was lost at sea and another was "badly broken."

Dorothea, according to Tiffany, was disappointed and "sad," for she "did not at all enjoy the reversed situation of a life-saving outfit that needed to be saved itself." She promptly gave directions for the broken boat, as well as the one that had disappeared but was later picked up, to be sent back to New York for thorough repair. It was not until the ensuing October that, in two detachments, the entire outfit landed back on Sable Island.

Dorothea received the first news of the behavior of the new little fleet from the Honorable Hugh Bell, chairman of the Board of Works in Halifax, who described how the boats had come to the rescue of a large American ship from Antwerp, with 160 passengers aboard. Bell wrote it "was cast upon one of the sandbanks off the northeast end of the island and lurched so that the sea beat into her and rendered all chance of escape by the efforts of the people on board quite hopeless. The sea was so heavy, and the weather so boisterous, that none of the island's boats could live in it."

He then said: "To reach the wreck from the station was over twenty miles; your wagons thus came into use. Your 'Reliance' rode over the waves, as the sailors said, like a duck, and with her and two of your smaller boats, the 'Samaritan' and the 'Rescue,' the whole of the passengers were safely landed; poor things, almost in a state of nudity, not being able to save anything from the ship. Will you not rejoice at this result of your bounty? Including the crew, one hundred and eighty human beings were saved by the means thus opportunely, and may I not add providentially, furnished through your care." He signed the letter, "I am very truly your friend and obedient servant, Hugh Bell."

A few weeks later he sent her a letter he had received on December 6, 1854, from Captain M. D. McKenna, superintendent of the Relief Station at Sable Island. The letter described how the *Reliance* had come to the rescue of the crippled ship the *Arcadia*, stuck on the southeast side of the northeast bar of the island in a dense fog and high wind. The *Reliance* made six trips to the wreck and brought on shore about eighty persons; the next day, it sailed out and landed the rest of the passengers and crew.

"The Francis metallic lifeboat 'Reliance' has done what no other boat could do, that I have ever seen," Captain McKenna reported:

> *It was a fearful time, yet the boats' crew each took their stations readily, and soon showed that they felt the "Reliance" to be worthy of her name.*
>
> *I am sure that our benevolent friend, Miss Dix, will feel herself more than compensated for her great exertions in behalf of Sable Island Establishment, when she becomes acquainted with what we have already done through the means she furnished, and we, with many others, have reason to thank God that her good works have been felt on Sable Island. For my own part I shall think of her with feelings of gratitude while memory lasts.*

Congratulatory letters from friends at home and in England were sent to Dorothea. On March 6, 1855, she received a letter from Lucy S. Adams in Castine, Maine, addressing her as "My Friend and Benefactress," and explaining: "You will not be surprised at this address when I tell you that my son was one of the crew of the ship 'Arcadia,' saved through your instrumentality. While our hearts ascend, I trust, to our Heavenly Preserver with grateful emotions, it is fitting that we should express to you our thanks and kind regards, with the hope that your benevolent efforts for elevating character and saving life may be crowned with success, and that the blessing of many ready to perish may come upon you."

This was the only time Dorothea did not engage her full efforts in helping the mentally ill. She took part in this one experiment to save the lives of those who would otherwise have drowned and then returned to her earlier quest to save the mental lives of the insane poor, the mission her heart most deeply championed.

She worked in the South from late autumn until spring. When the heat became too intense in Boston, she transferred her activity to regions as far to the northeast as Halifax, Nova Scotia, where she worked toward the foundation of a much-needed asylum for the insane. In Halifax, the Honorable Hugh Bell helped her with untiring courage and devotion. His admiration for her ran deep. He called her "Minerva" and "Telemachus." Minerva was the Roman goddess of wisdom, technical skill, and invention, Telemachus, the warrior son of Odysseus and Penelope.

Bell wrote her on July 5, 1853: "Your vigorous, unwavering faith and your firm, unflinching resolution shame away doubt and inspire confidence. . . . We shall conquer yet!"

He was able to write in triumph later in 1853: "The session of our Legislature closed yesterday, and I hasten to inform you that *something* has been done for our long and earnest effort: £15,000 equal to $60,000 has been appropriated, with the condition that £5,000 more be subscribed. . . . They have made me, officially, the acting and chief commissioner. How strangely and unexpectedly are things brought about! . . . I am bound in gratitude to be thankful that Providence has blessed my humble efforts in behalf of our afflicted fellow beings. . . . I cannot but think how much stronger your faith was than mine. You always said it would be done. I confess that I had given up hope, during my life."

With the opening of the Congressional session of 1854, the signs looked favorable for renewing Dorothea's national campaign. The excitement in the Democratic party over the land issue had subsided, and her triumphs in so many states impressed Congress.

Again five thousand copies of her *Memorial* were printed as her supporters stopped at the library to assure her that her cause seemed "promising."

The first victory came on March 9, 1854, when her bill, introduced for the fifth time in six years, passed the Senate once more by a large majority. She wrote Anne on March 9, 1854: "Yours this morning received just when I was putting pen to paper to tell you that my bill has passed the Senate by more than two thirds majority, 25 to 12. Congratulations flow in. I, in my heart, think the very opponents are glad; and, as I rejoice quietly and silently, I feel that it is 'the Lord who has made my mountain to stand strong.'"

In August, the House of Representatives passed the bill, 98 to 84. Success was then secured in both houses in the same session, as required. The bill now awaited the signature of the new president, Franklin Pierce, to become law.

Congratulations flowed in. Dr. Thomas S. Kirkbride, who had worked many years in behalf of the insane, had written Dorothea four years before that he possessed "full confidence your bill will pass, and nothing but the supreme selfishness of politicians—which is genuine insanity as to the welfare of the country, of the very worst kind—keeps Congress from doing some good acts which would tend to redeem them in the estimation of the people." Now he rejoicingly wrote, "A thousand congratulations in the success of your noble, disinterested and persevering efforts! There is some virtue yet in Congress, and a large hope for the Republic."

It seemed that Dorothea's most cherished wish would finally be granted. Letters poured in from all over the country congratulating her. She would no longer have to spend long and weary hours wrestling with successive state legislatures. She could, as Tiffany put it, receive "honorable discharge from the service," rest, and write the story of her life, as Dr. Bell had suggested.

But suddenly an unexpected lightning bolt of words fell on the bill, obliterating it. President Pierce vetoed it. Dorothea's long struggle to have it passed, the agony of six years of hard work, were blown to the winds.

At first, Dorothea could not believe what happened. She insisted that President Pierce had personally told her of his interest in the bill, which twice in the past six years had passed both the House and the Senate.

At the first rumor of an impending veto, Dr. Kirkbride had written her, "Is it possible that the President can really think of vetoing your bill? If he does, ought he not expect to see the ghosts of insane people around his bed at night, as long as he lives?" William Darlington, of Pennsylvania, wrote that he had "lost all patience with those narrow-minded, caviling demagogues who everlastingly plead the Constitution against every generous measure, and recklessly trample it under foot whenever it stands in the way of their selfish purposes and foregone conclusions."

President Pierce explained his objections to the 12,225,000 Acre Bill in his veto message. Starting with the declaration that he had "been compelled to resist the deep sympathies of my own heart in favor of the humane purposes sought to be accomplished," he said that Congress had the power to make provisions of an eleemosynary character only within the limits of the District of Columbia.

He pointed out that Congress had crossed this line on two previous occasions, in Kentucky and Connecticut, in favor of the indigent blind and the indigent deaf and mute, transcending its powers and setting unsafe precedents—examples to be avoided, rather than followed, he maintained.

The president stated further, "If Congress have power to make provisions for the indigent insane *without the limits of this district*, it has the same power to provide for the indigent who are not insane, and thus to transfer to the federal government the charge of *all the poor in all the States*."

He added, "The fountains of charity will be dried up at home, and the several States, instead of bestowing their own means on the social wants of their own people, may themselves become humble suppliants for the bounty of the federal government, reversing their true relation to this Union."

Many senators thought that President Pierce's explanation made it difficult to account for his act on any ground other than that of his personal idiosyncrasies of character and opinion. It was the veto of a biased man, they believed, not that of an honored public official.

President Pierce was known to be an alcoholic and was not chosen for a second term.

He was also described as a man who had an almost virulent hatred of everything savoring of what he called "sentimental legislation," meaning helping the poor and the insane. Elected president on the avowed platform of a "Northern man with Southern principles," in the national issue between freedom and slavery he insisted that a deaf ear be turned to anything but the plea for the most narrow and bald construction of the letter of the Constitution. A man like this would be against Dorothea's proposal from the first word. He would believe that to help the indigent insane meant supporting every sick man, every vagabond, every drunkard in the country. He would look on Dorothea's bill as an evil befalling the nation.

Dorothea finally accepted in sorrow the realization that the president had vetoed her bill. She called her most powerful supporters and asked if there were any possibility of carrying the bill over the presidential veto by a two-thirds majority. They sadly told her that it was not possible. To cross the will of the president meant political death.

Though defeated, she could not help but feel she had put up a good fight. One man, unfortunately the man at the top, had killed the bill she had hoped with the deepest part of her heart would pass.

But at least she had set a blueprint. She could feel pride that both the Senate and the House of Representatives had championed her cherished idea.

6

REFORMS ACROSS THE SEA

Dorothea's life had been one of drastic losses. First, her beloved grandfather had died when she was seven, followed in later years by her father, her mother, and her grandmother. In a way, the loss of the congressional bill that would have helped so many unfortunate men, women, and children was like losing all of them, too, for now they would not receive the care that might have returned them to normalcy.

She felt defeated, as though she needed to recuperate once again in a far country. She set out to see her dear English friends, the Rathbones of Liverpool, with whom she had been communicating over the years. She also planned to visit some of the asylums of Europe, to learn from them whatever might be of future use in America. She would spend as much time abroad as she needed to recover from the bereavement caused by President Pierce's unhappy veto of the 12,225,000 Acres Bill.

Early in September 1854, Dorothea set sail for Liverpool on the *Arctic*—an ill-fated steamship that, on the return voyage, would sink to the bottom of the Atlantic, drowning almost everyone on board. An incident connected to her leaving appeared in the *New York Daily Tribune* of September 11, written by a reporter. It read:

> *I happened to be in the office of the American steam packets when Miss Dix called to pay her passage. The clerk handed her a receipt, but declined the money, saying that Mr. E. K. Collins (the chief owner of the line) had directed him to request her acceptance of the passage. With much emotion, Miss Dix acknowledged her obligation to Mr. Collins, adding that the sum thus returned to her would enable her to carry out a plan she had much at heart.*
>
> *On board the ship, Miss Dix learned that she had yet more for which to thank Mr. Collins. He had ordered that no one else should be put in her stateroom, thus presenting her with two passages. He was on board when she arrived. She approached to tender her thanks, but, taking her hands in his with an emotion that did him honor, he said, "The nation, madam, owes you a debt of gratitude which it can never repay, and of which I, as an individual, am only too happy to be thus privileged to mark my sense."*
>
> *Miss Dix could only reply with tears, for, as was evident to all who saw her, her nervous system is completely prostrated. Could we expect it to be otherwise, in view of her immense labors and her grievous disappointments!*

For many years it had been the habit of railway companies all over the Union to send her yearly passes and of express companies to forward, free of charge, all the objects she was unceasingly collecting for prisons, hospitals, and insane asylums.

She wrote Anne aboard the *Arctic* on September 11, 1854:

"I pass the time with such a measure of listlessness as affords but few results that will tell for others' good. However, I give you an example of my success. I had observed on Sunday several parties betting on the steamer's run. I waited till the bets were decided, and then asked the winner for the winnings, which I put into the captain's care for 'The Home for the Children of Indigent Sailors' in New York. Tonight I am going to ask each passenger for a donation for the same object, as our thank offering for preservation thus far on our voyage. I shall, I think, get above $150."

Weary and downcast as she might feel, she still worked in behalf of the needy. For six weeks after her arrival in Liverpool, she stayed with the Rathbones. She rested part of the time and made excursions into the country to see the changing fall colors of flowers and trees, one way of soothing herself.

Then her mind returned fully to the most important mission in her life as she wrote Anne on September 21: "I am still here with dear friends, much occupied with charitable institutions and the meetings of the British Scientific Association. All this tires me sadly, but I shall take things easier in a week. It is my purpose to go to Scotland to see the hospitals in ten days."

She deferred that visit for a few weeks, enjoying herself in Ireland. She wrote Mrs. Rathbone on October 25, describing her experiences from seven in the evening to four in the morning:

> *I reached Parsontown yesterday at two P.M. Sent a note of introduction to the Castle, to Lord Rosse, asking permission to see his telescope. In half an hour received an invitation to dinner at seven P.M.; and almost immediately his assistant, Mr. Mitchell, arrived at the Parsontown Arms, to say that Lord Rosse had sent him to conduct me to the Castle, in order that the instruments might be seen by day and the machinery. I reserve all details till we meet, simply saying that I was swinging in mid-air, sixty feet from the ground, at two in the morning, yesterday, along with Lord Rosse, Captain King, Mr. Mitchell and Mr. Tirn, looking down on a massive gallery through the most magnificent telescope in the world.*

Such was the psychic medicine she applied to the mental wounds caused by President Pierce. She wrote Anne on November 16, 1854, after a tour of Ireland, which she enjoyed for four weeks, "a period which I shall always recall with lively interest," that she now wanted to become familiar with the institutions of England, including the literary, scientific, and humane.

For the first time, perhaps in her whole life, she felt free to explore the scenery of new countries and to forget for the moment her wish to help the unhappy impoverished inmates of asylums. But then on December 8, she wrote Anne, "I could not but smile at your idea of my visiting the prisons in Italy, an idea, certainly, that you have the sole merit of suggesting, for it had not occurred to me, for any purpose, to penetrate into those places of so many bitter memories and horrible sufferings."

She then asked, "What should I gain, or what would others gain, by my passage through those dreary dungeons and under the Piombini? When I do visit prisons, it is where I have before me a rational object and a clear purpose. As I write, the little birds are singing 'merrily, cheerily' below my windows, the flowers on my table yield a sweet fragrance, the lauristinas open their buds and flowers along the walks, and the grass is a vivid green."

But by February 26, 1855, Dorothea was in Edinburgh, Scotland, writing Anne once again about the needed reforms in the treatment of the indigent insane:

> *I have had the good fortune to enjoy the best society here, and shall recollect so much with great pleasure that it is painful to connect with it what is very much the reverse of good,—I mean a few of the many public institutions in the city and neighborhood, which are predominantly bad. Of these none are so much needing quick reform as the private establishments for the insane. I am confident that this move is to rest with me, and that the sooner I address myself to this work of humanity, the sooner will my conscience cease to suggest effort, or rebuke inaction.*
>
> *It will be no holiday work, however; but hundreds of miserable creatures may be released from a bitter bondage, which the people at large are quite unconscious of. It is true I came here for pleasure, but that is no reason why I should close my eyes to the condition of these most helpless of all God's creatures.*

Dorothea showed the true spirit of crusaders for a cause in which they fervently believe. She no longer felt crushed by the savage defeat of her congressional bill by a president who had no understanding of those in need of mental health. Once again she put defeat behind her, now on the march to rescue those who lacked sanity for the moment.

Mrs. Rathbone wrote Dorothea in Edinburgh that, for the time being, she should not allow work to interfere with her need to recuperate. Dorothea replied at once, carefully describing her feelings:

> *I am not so very ill, only very variable, and, I assure you, do not work the more for being tired. I am not naturally very active, and never do anything there is a fair chance other people will take up. So, when you know I am busy, you may be sure it is leading the forlorn hope,—which I conduct to a successful termination through a certain sort of obstinacy that some people make the blunder of calling zeal, and the yet greater blunder of having its first inciting cause in philanthropy. I have no particular love for my species at large, but own to an exhaustless fund of compassion.*
>
> *It is pretty clear that I am in for a serious work in both England and Scotland. I do not see the end of this beginning, but everybody says, who speaks at all on this question, that if I go away the whole work will fall off. So I pursue what I so strangely commenced.*

Dorothea was saying that what she felt about the unfortunate indigent insane was not limited to America, that her concern was worldwide—being poor and insane had no national boundaries, it was the human being, not the American or the Canadian, who suffered.

Several doctors in London, who heard of her amazing achievements in America, sought her out. A Dr. Simpson introduced her as "our timely-arrived benefactor and reformer." Dorothea told Mrs. Rathbone that she felt she had "passed the Rubicon and retreat is not to be thought of."

In his *History of the Insane in the British Isles*, Dr. Daniel Hack Tuke, a descendent of William Tuke, one of the most prominent psychiatrists of Great Britain, wrote in 1882 that in Scotland Dorothea revolutionized the lunacy laws of the land. He was an eyewitness to her work there. He said her earlier work "no doubt to some extent prepared the way for the victory Miss Dix achieved."

He spoke of Dorothea's contributions to Scotland:

> *A well-known American lady, Miss Dix, who devoted her life to the interests of the insane, visited Scotland, and I had the opportunity of hearing from her own lips, on her return from her philanthropic expedition, the narration of what she saw of the cruel neglect of the pauper lunatics in that country. She caused so much sensation by her visits and her remonstrances that a certain official in Edinburgh decided to anticipate "the American Invader," as Dr. W. A. F. Browne called her.*
>
> *Miss Dix was, however, equal to the occasion, and hurriedly leaving the scene of her investigations, she took the night mail to London, and appeared before the Home Secretary on the following day, when the gentleman from Edinburgh was still on the road, quite unconscious that the good lady had already traversed it. The facts she laid before the Home Office were so startling that they produced a marked effect, and, notwithstanding counter allegations, the conclusion was very soon arrived at that there was sufficient* prima facie *evidence to justify an inquiry. A Royal Commission was appointed, dated April 3, 1855, to inquire into the condition of lunatic asylums in Scotland, and the existing state of the law of that country in reference to lunatics and lunatic asylums.*

By April 9, 1855, two months after Dorothea's arrival in Scotland, Queen Victoria appointed several of Her Majesty's commissioners to look into the state of the "Lunatic Asylums in Scotland" and "into the present state of the law respecting Lunatics and Lunatic Asylums in that part of the United Kingdom."

In giving a speech at the House of Commons, a Mr. Ellice, M.P. (Member of Parliament) reported:

> *The Commission was entirely due to Miss Dix's exertion. After visiting the lunatic asylums of England, she proceeded to Scotland, where her suspicions were aroused by*

the great difficulty she experienced in penetrating into the lunatic asylums of Scotland; but when she did gain access, she found the unfortunate inmates were in a most miserable condition.

She came to London and placed herself in communication with the Secretary of State for the Home Department and with the Duke of Argyll, and at her instance and without any public movement on the subject, a Royal Commission was appointed to inquire into the state of the lunatic asylums of Scotland. No one, we feel sure, could read the Report of the Commission without feeling grateful to that lady for having been instrumental in exposing proceedings which were disgraceful to this or any civilized country.

Setting to work on the issues opened to them by Dorothea, the members of the Royal Commission realized the fidelity of the revelation of the shame and cruelty she had so impressively made. Dr. David Skae, of the Royal Edinburgh Asylum for the Insane, wrote her, expressing his amazement at her power to impress influential people, insisting she was indispensable in the area for which she campaigned.

Not before 1857, almost a year after she returned to the United States, did the commission make its report to Parliament, revealing "that an appalling amount of misery prevails throughout Scotland," when it came to lunatic asylums. The details furnished by the commission "form only a part of the picture of misery; and had we been able to extend our investigations, it would, we are convinced, have assumed a much darker shade," the report concluded.

On August 25, 1857, Parliament passed an act through which a new epoch was inaugurated in the humane and adequate provision of care for the insane, especially the pauper insane, of Scotland. Money was raised for the founding of new and humanely administered asylums in various parts of the land.

Dorothea by then had returned to the United States, but she received several letters from men in England and Scotland, thanking her for uncovering the horrors in Scotland. Sir James A. Clark, physician to the queen, who had attended Dorothea during a severe inflammatory attack in London, wrote from Bagshot Park, Surrey, on December 30, 1861:

"Before going farther, I will give you a piece of information which I feel sure will gratify you, as the first movement in the improvement which has been effected in Scotland through your exertions. The treatment of the pauper insane in Scotland is now more carefully attended to than in any other part of Great Britain, I may say."

Dr. Tuke, in whose house at Falmouth, Cornwall, England, Dorothy had sought rest at one point when she returned from Scotland, sent his congratulations in a short but pungent note: "I think you might say to the Scotch, 'You are my joy and my crown,' for they have gone on wonderfully since 'The American Invader' aroused them from their lethargy."

Before she left England for the Continent, Dorothea had learned of the pathetic conditions for the insane in the Channel Islands, located in the British Channel and politically attached to Great Britain but connected with France by their geographic position. The largest islands were Jersey, Guernsey, and Alderney.

When Dorothea had been in Edinburgh, a woman from the south of England, hearing her name and knowing of her work, suggested that she visit Jersey and Guernsey because of the severe abuses inflicted on the insane. She had begged Dorothea to hurry there at once.

When she left England, Dorothea wrote Anne on June 1, 1855, that she hoped soon to "get to the Channel Islands, Jersey and Guernsey, with God's blessing. I was at a very good hotel, but my friends, Dr. and Mrs. Tuke, insisted on my removal to their nice comfortable home, where I am tended as carefully and tenderly as if I were a sister. I have been very feeble, but not helpless, and never cheerless. It is now beginning to *dawn* on me that I may not go to the United States this autumn. I do not see any great use in getting back just as the cold weather advances, unless there is a call to labor. If so, I dare say the strength would come for the 'daily task,'—'daily the manna fell from heaven.' "

She concluded, "I should like one of your sweet nice letters now and then. Cannot you give me so much pleasure?"

From Dr. D. H. Van Leuven's letters, Dorothea knew one thing was clear: There was evidence that the hue and cry raised in England

and Scotland over miscreants working in private madhou____.... mercenary ends and with nefarious and criminal intent was a reality.

With this sorry situation in mind, she set out to visit the island of Jersey in mid-July 1855. She was no longer a single woman dependent on her own resources, as when she entered Scotland, but now was known to have had the ear of the lord chancellor and the home secretary, as well as the prestige of parliamentary success.

She first met young Dr. Van Leuven, who had sent Dr. Tuke the report that brought her there. She wrote of this visit to Dr. Buttolph, superintendent at the asylum in Trenton, from 8 Queen's Terrace, St. Helliers, Jersey, on July 15: "My dear Friend,—I now proceed to give you a running narrative of my affairs here. Left London, Friday . . . detained off Guernsey by fogs, just escaped the sunken rocks, and landed four and a half hours late at the Jersey pier on Saturday, 5 P.M.

"Sunday, at home all day. Monday, 9 A.M., took a carriage and drove with Dr. Van Leuven to the hospital—found the insane in a horrid state, naked, filthy, and attended by persons of ill character committed to this establishment for vice too gross to admit of their being at large."

She inspected the forty insane men and women in the cells and yards, then was driven with a letter of introduction in hand to Government House. The governor was not at home but she left a note, previously prepared, asking for an interview "at His Excellency's convenience." She had lunch and at three o'clock drove to look at a site for "the" hospital les Moraines, property of an insane woman who died without heirs, from which the Crown derived a large annual rent.

She also visited several insane persons in private families, which she described as "a sad, very sad scene." During her absence, the governor had called, asking her to come to his office at ten the next morning and to join him for dinner that evening. General Tonzel had also called, leaving his number and an invitation for breakfast. Early in the morning she went to the general's home, where they talked about business affairs as they ate. At ten he drove with her to see the governor, who, after hearing of her work in America and England, promised her governmental support in his area.

Dorothea wrote Mrs. Rathbone of her achievements, knowing

that she and her husband would want to learn of her progress. First, she said, she had managed to get the villain, a "Mr. Pothecary," into the custody of the high constable of Jersey by order of the governor and counsel of the attorney general.

She added: "So *that* business is well settled, and the laws will protect the patients Pothecary has so boldly *transported*. I have seen them. Next, I have got a farm for the hospital that I hope shall be, and the hospital I will call La Maison de l'Espérance. I shall stay in Jersey so long as will settle the question of hospital or no hospital."

One other letter from Dorothea to Dr. Buttolph constituted her only other correspondence from Jersey. Written July 18, 1855, it reported: "At a full committee of sixteen gentlemen yesterday, the resolution was passed *unanimously* to build a hospital here for the insane, with the least possible delay. To-morrow, I accompany a subcommittee to search out a fit site and farm, and a structure for 100 patients is to be commenced upon a plan capable of extension at need. . . . I want hints, plans, and specifications from you, *without cost*. Let me hear by return steamer. I must push these people, or the building will not be finished till next century. . . . I expect to go to Guernsey on Friday, and to England on Monday next."

She returned to her friends in Greenbank, England, where she wrote Anne: "Safely arrived in the dear old home. I rest and am quiet to my heart's content. Friends are all well and in prosperity and so I find them drawing toward the latter days in peace, doing good to all as they have opportunity."

Dr. Tuke congratulated her on her work in Jersey, writing: "I think you have good reason to be satisfied with the results already apparent, and with Dr. Van Leuven left on the spot, there is probably less danger of the thing being lost sight of. There will be nothing more needed, I believe, but keeping up a brisk fire."

It was not, however, until nearly thirty-five years later that a large public asylum was finally completed for the humane and scientific treatment of the insane on the island of Jersey. But at least Dorothea had started them on their way.

The nature and degree of the impression produced on the minds of Dorothea's truest friends at this triumphant period of her life was expressed by her host, William Rathbone. Dorothea had been taken to his home when she fell dangerously ill, the victim of lung disease, on her first visit to England in 1837. Through the successful years of her later work in the United States, both Mr. and Mrs. Rathbone followed her achievements with deep interest, writing her letters and, in turn, receiving hers. They now witnessed the wonders she had accomplished in Scotland and on the island of Jersey.

Mr. Rathbone wrote from Greenbank on July 8, 1855, when she was staying with the Tukes just before she left for home:

> *My dear Friend,—Not being inclined to sleep, I have thought that a quiet hour before breakfast could not be better employed than in saying, God bless my valued and loved friend, and speed her successfully in her progress— so far as is consistent with the scheme of His inscrutable, yet ever beneficent, Providence! He has* tried *you in the success of what you have undertaken beyond what I have ever known, or, as far as my recollection serves me, have read of any other person, male or female.*
>
> *I speak now of the entirety of the success as much as of the extent, and it has not turned your head or, as I believe, led you to forget the source from which your strength has been derived. . . . That your head has not been turned to the magnitude and vast extent of your success, is, as much of the many other parts of your character, the subject of my respectful admiration.*

He signed the letter, "your affectionate friend, W. Rathbone." She could also enjoy the testimonials paid her by many large public bodies, including twenty state legislatures in America, the Congress of the United States, and now the British Parliament. Her life, for the most part, was lonely and filled with physical pain, yet she had achieved successes that no one before had been able to carry out and had been praised by men in the highest political bodies of the world.

As her friend Rathbone said, "God has *tried* you in the success of what you have undertaken beyond what I have ever known, or, as far as my recollection serves me, have read of any other person, male or female."

That she had aroused the praise of Americans abroad appeared in a letter to a friend in England written by Mrs. E. H. Walsh, wife of the American ambassador to France, sent from Versailles, June 3, 1885: "Pray remember me to Miss Dix. If she is with you, tell her I kiss the hem of her garment, and bless God that our country has produced such a noble heart. She will see the honorable mention of her services by the Earl of Shaftesbury in Parliament, and Mr. Walsh is about to add his testimony to her immense worth, in his correspondence. He regrets very much not having made the acquaintance of Miss Dix. He is right. Such a woman is to be worshiped, if anything human could be worshiped."

The Annual Convention of the Association of Superintendents of American Insane Asylums, held in summer 1855, passed the following resolution and sent it to Dorothea:

> Resolved, *That the Secretary of the Association be directed to request Miss Dix to favor us at our next meeting with an account of her observations and investigations in the countries she is now visiting. . . . Our Association has never met without many grateful recognitions of your invaluable services to humanity. . . . I can assure you that you never held a higher place in our most respectful consideration.*
>
> *It is to our liveliest satisfaction to learn that our mother-countrymen have received you with that eminent consideration and personal kindness which are so fully accorded to you everywhere at home. We all miss you from the country, and especially do those of us miss the great benefits of your personal encouragement and cooperation, who are the immediate masters of those "many mansions" of beneficence, which owe their existence under Providence to the extraordinary success of your appeals to humanity in prosperity in favor of humanity in adversity. We pray for the renewal of your health and strength, and shall hail with gladness your return to the scenes of your widest and most fruitful labors.*

The superintendent of one of the large asylums in America wrote her: "It is not, however, by any such visible tokens as books and pictures that your visit will be remembered. Your clear and unmistakable showing of what our defects are, is the greatest boon that you could have conferred. I did not misunderstand those criticisms, so delicately administered to others, and, at the same time, so applicable to us. Not only has every observation been carefully treasured up in my memory, every word which could be remembered has been made the text for suggestive commentaries of my own."

Another eminent professional, whose name also was not made public, wrote that he had not been

> *idle during your absence from the country upwards of six months, but have diligently striven to do what was demanded of my position,—and what I thought you would approve,—always feeling a responsibility to your prospective approbation in carrying on a work which is so rightfully yours. If you can say, 'Well done!' to what is already done, I shall be glad. Your confidence and friendship are a well of pleasure and a tower of strength to me.*
>
> *I am not unaware of your noble and extraordinary achievements in view of the amelioration of the condition of the insane in Scotland. I know that this is a secondary consideration with you, but I think the narrative of that achievement will make one of the brightest pages in the history of the progressive ameliorations of the sufferings of humanity.*

In spite of her fatigue and her wish to rest completely for a while, Dorothea's passion for helping those who were unable to help themselves and who, as a result, were punished and denigrated, once again proved stronger than her wish to enjoy the scenic old-world splendor of countries across the Atlantic.

She wanted to visit parts of Europe that lay to the east and south. Such a visit had not been possible on her first trip abroad because she had been so ill. She was now in good enough health to leave England and to explore the fascinating countries to the east. She intended to go for both work and pleasure.

7

TACKLING THE CONTINENT

Dorothea wrote Anne from East Riding, England, on June 1, 1855, that she did not see any "great use" in returning to the United States "just as the cold weather advances, unless there is a call to labor. If so, I dare say the strength would come for the daily task."

In late summer she received an invitation from the Rathbones, who were vacationing in Switzerland, to join them as their guest and enjoy the Alps. The Rathbones suggested, because of her ill health, that she should bring a capable woman as her maid.

She replied in her characteristic way:

> You desire that I should have some one with me, a maid, to save me fatigue and prevent my feeling desolate when alone. A maid would be only in the way, with nothing to do; and, for feeling desolate, I never felt desolate in my life, and I have been much alone in both populous and thinly-settled countries.
>
> You are quite right in saying I cannot rest in England

*any more than in America, now that I know how much
suffering calls aloud for relief. I must turn a deaf ear to the
cries and go beyond the reach of the sound of the many
afflicted ones, till I have gathered up force to renew—
should it please God that I work longer—the work where-
unto I am called.*

She accepted the Rathbones' generous invitation and headed for
the Alps in Switzerland. She exulted in what she described as the
"snow-clad peaks mantled with their regal robes of pasture and
forest, as a sublime cathedral anthem to God." Her deep interest in
nature also took her to fields of flowers. Later, during her work in the
Civil War, she would write the Rathbones in 1862: "Your thoughtful
care for my gratification in planning that journey to the Continent
has enriched my life for all time. I never find the glorious view of the
Alps fade from my mind's eye. A thousand incidents recall and repeat
the memory of those grand snow peaks piercing the skies."

She rested for a while, enjoyed nature's beauties, felt revived. She
then decided to carry out a plan that had been steadily growing
stronger—to take an extended tour of hospitals, insane asylums,
and prisons of Europe, including Turkey. She thought she might
visit Palestine, farther to the east, a place she ardently wished
to see.

She accompanied the Rathbones back to England, then boarded a
ship to France. She preferred being alone when absorbed in work.
She spoke only English, except for a smattering of French, but also
planned to visit Italy, Greece, Turkey, Russia, Germany, Norway,
and Holland.

Tiffany traced a number of her letters written at this time as he
followed Dorothea's trail through her journeys in Europe, to which
she devoted nearly one year. She wrote Mrs. Rathbone from Mettray, near Tours, on September 3, 1855: "Visited hospitals for aged
men and women, and establishment for juvenile offenders at Quilly,
five miles out of Rouen, at St. Yon. Then Paris, Orleans, Blois, Tours
and Mettray. Go next to Nantes, return to Paris."

Also during September, no date noted, she wrote: "Yesterday, and
only till then, I became possessor of a full Police and Magisterial
Sanction under seal,—for which nine official parties were to be

reached,—for entering all the prisons and hospitals of Paris, without exception."

In November, undated, she wrote Mrs. Torrey in Boston:

> *I am still entirely occupied in seeing the charitable institutions of this city and environs, which I hope to have done by two weeks more. The very short days and the very dull weather unite to make this slow work. I am obliged to take much rest; it seems to have become absolutely the condition on which I do anything in the pursuit of my vocation. The vast multiplication of all sorts of hospitals for all sorts of complaints and infirmities and for all ages, tells of the different conditions of family life from that we are used to observe. I quite comprehend the turbulence and crimes of revolutionary periods, especially those movements in which women have been conspicuous for trampling on all laws human and divine.*

From Paris she wrote Dr. Buttolph, in Trenton, New Jersey, on December 3, 1855:

> *I should say that all the charitable institutions of Paris, liberally supported as they are by government, possess in a large measure great excellencies, but two radical universal defects, at least, strike the most casual observer. The want of ventilation is the chiefest ill, and quite explains the amazing mortality, apart from the well-known experimental methods of treatment by the* Internes—*resident students. In all these establishments, associated with other employees, are found Sisters of Charity, and nuns of various orders. Some of them are very self-denying, not many. They are never over-tasked, except possibly in some period of serious epidemic. As for the priests, they should for the most part occupy places in homes of correctional discipline, and enlightening cultivation.*

In the second week of January, Dorothea completed her examination of the charitable institutions of France and left for Italy. She wrote Mrs. Rathbone from Genoa on March 3, 1856:

*This morning I spent in the hospital for the insane, and
find much to commend, with some things to disapprove;
but after seeing that at Rome, I regard all other institutions in this country with comparative favor. . . .*

*I left Naples, Rome and Florence with regret that I could
not have had leisure to observe the works of art, ancient
and modern, which have great attraction, but I saw a
good deal, considering the claims of hospitals and the
short time I spent in each place. I get daily news from
Constantinople which moves my sympathy for the poor
insane of Turkey. Innovations in usages are now fast
going on there, so we may hope the hospitals will share in
the advance of civilization.*

Three days later, Dorothea wrote Mrs. Torrey, describing her trip
to Italy, saying she had "found at Rome a hospital for the insane so
very bad, that I set about the difficult work of reform at once, and
during the fourteen days I was there, so far succeeded as to have
Papal promises and Cardinal assurances, etc., of immediate action in
remedying abuses and supplying deficiencies. . . . I also wish a new
hospital in Florence. This has been contemplated by the Commune
of Florence, but the onerous taxation consequent on the Austrian
invasion, has impoverished the city."

She spoke of leaving shortly for Constantinople, believing that
reform was needed there, and saying, "My work seems to me to be
indicated by Providence, and I cannot conscientiously turn away
from attempting, as far as possible, to alleviate miseries wherever I
find them." She had lived with many miseries as a child and grown
up with the hope of alleviating them.

Four days later, she again wrote Mrs. Rathbone from Turin, Italy,
saying it was just as easy traveling alone in Europe as in England or
America. She described the hospitals for the insane as "so bad that I
feel quite heartsick. . . . I do not think it will do much good, but it is
my duty to try. I shall appeal in writing to the king."

She added that her plans appeared to be "about as stable as spring
breezes." She said that she had not only to convince officers of the
government, but to make a stand against "the *priests*, who interfere
with everything that is done or to be done. I never felt anything

more difficult than this work in Italy. In Rome I found government and the priestly office united, and the very *shame* of foreign and Protestant interposition quickened them to action or *promise* rather than humanity; but in Florence, Genoa, and here, it is a fact that changes are coming over the old rule, and one must wait a little where so much is doing and to be done."

In another letter to Dr. and Mrs. Buttolph, she wrote that in Rome, "6,000 priests, 300 monks, 3,000 nuns, and a spiritual sovereignty joined with the temporal powers" had not assured "for the miserable insane a decent, much less an intelligent, care." She added, "I could not bear to know this and do nothing. An appeal to the Pope [Pope Pius IX], which involved, care, patience, time, and negotiation has secured but promises. . . . Since coming to Florence five days ago, I find a bad hospital there, and mountains of difficulty in the way of remedy for serious ills. I have the idea of removing these mountains, and seeing if Protestant energy cannot work what Catholic powers fail to undertake."

She found an ally in Cardinal Antonelli, an intellectual man who sympathized with her and backed her suggestions. She believed he was the most enlightened, humane, and merciful man she found in Rome, one who would work in behalf of the wronged and suffering indigent insane.

Pope Pius IX, who spoke English, listened to her plea, was shocked at what she had found, and drove unannounced to the insane asylum to see the conditions for himself. When he met Dorothea again, he said he was distressed at the conditions and warmly thanked her for crossing the seas and calling them to his attention. When someone later asked, "Did you really kneel down and kiss his hand?" she replied, "Most certainly I did. I revered him for his saintliness."

She later learned that the Pope had taken steps to erect a new asylum "on the most approved plan." Her friend Mrs. Bancroft visited Naples and wrote her on February 7, 1876, twenty-one years later, knowing of her interest in what had happened, that a new asylum had been created by Pope Pius IX, "which your efforts originated in his mind," and that there were 650 patients, though two obstacles were in the way. She listed them as "poverty" and the "lack of the best experience" in how to handle the patients. She concluded that the present institution proved a "great revolution in the care and treatment of the insane, in comparison with former methods," even though the Pope lacked the means to make the place as pleasant and inviting as "money" might provide.

Dorothea could take credit for the beginning of change in the care of the indigent insane in Italy. She had started a trail that began in England, wound into France, and now covered Italy, as she prepared to sail for Greece.

Dorothea left Italy early in March 1856 to head farther east. The Crimean War between Russia and England, France, and Turkey was still being waged after two years. Everyone praised Florence Nightingale, the "cheering angel," as the British called her, who took care of the wounded on the field and brought nurses from England.

In another letter to Dr. Buttolph, written as her steamer lay at anchor in the harbor of the island of Corfu, she said: "You will not be more surprised than I am that I find traveling *alone* perfectly easy. I get into all the hospitals and prisons that I have time to see or strength to explore. I take no refusals, and yet I speak neither German, Italian, Greek, or Schlavonic [Slavic]. I have no letter of introduction, and know no persons *en route*. I found at Trieste a very bad hospital for the insane. Fortunately a physician attached to the suite of Archduke Maximilian has promised the intervention of the government at Trieste and assured me that all the institutions of Austria shall be open to my visits if I come to Vienna."

Later in the month, on March 27, she wrote Mr. Rathbone from Corfu:

> *I have just time, since running on shore to see the prisons and hospitals, to report myself briefly to you and Mrs. R. Providence graciously protects me, and I am in no respects thus far impeded in my great objects of seeing the prisons and hospitals. By rare good fortune, I had an introduction to the physician of the Archduke Maximilian at Trieste, and made a move for a reform and*

renewal of the hospitals for the insane in that part of the Austrian Dominions; also the promise of the entrée to all the institutions of the Empire, if I went to Vienna. When the boat arrived last night, I went on shore as early as I could do anything, took a cab and drove to the Greek institutions;—saw all!

Five days later she awaited the arrival of a steamer at Piraeus, the port of Athens. She wrote Mrs. Rathbone on April 2, 1856:

I am waiting for the arrival of the steamer which came around the Peloponnesus. I came by the Isthmus that I might land at Aneona and the Ionian Islands to see the hospitals. I reached Athens at dark last night; left at noon to resume my sea voyage. The weather is intensely cold. Mt. Parnassus is as white as Mt. Blanc. . . .

This hour arrives a French steamer with the blessed news of Peace [the end of the Crimean War]. We give devout thanks that the hours of warfare are ended, but how long it must be before the wounds which have been inflicted on social and domestic happiness are healed or forgotten. . . .

I hoped after crossing the Isthmus to visit Corinth, but the captain would not consent to my leaving the protection of the powerful guard of one hundred which surrounded the transport carriages. As the danger was shown to be real, I readily gave up my previous wish. A fierce band of robbers attacked the carriage twenty days since, and succeeded in getting all the luggage and money, of which a large sum was being conveyed for paying the soldiers at Athens. So in each carriage sat an armed soldier, while at the side, in close file, rode a bodyguard who looked quite able to protect a much more valuable company. . . .

I have no idea how long I shall be in Constantinople, but everywhere I hear the most sad accounts of the insane there, on all the Islands, and in Asia Minor. I see if I can only secure something for Constantinople, it is all I ought to attempt, and of that I am not sanguine at all. I feel that

Miss Nightingale will have a great work still in the East.
God bless her efforts!

Dorothea reached Constantinople on April 10 and promptly
wrote Mrs. Rathbone:

> *I made most of the landings en route. At Smyrna I found*
> *a good English hospital for sailors, and also one for the*
> *Dutch and Greeks. . . . My only associates were two*
> *physicians,—one an Italian belonging to the ship, the*
> *other an Austrian from Vienna, highly educated, and of*
> *the most benevolent disposition. He was on his way to*
> *Jerusalem, to execute the will of a lady in Vienna, who had*
> *given 50,000 florins to establish a school for poor children*
> *in the Holy City. . . .*
> *After breakfast, I stepped into a caïque with two*
> *rowers,—speaking the words "Hospital! Scutari!"—and*
> *in half an hour landed at the wharf of upper Scutari. I*
> *paid and discharged the boatmen, and, inquiring of an*
> *English sailor the way to the nurses' quarter, proceeded*
> *thither. Miss Nightingale was absent, having been a*
> *month at Balaklava, where there is much sickness of the*
> *English and French troops.*
> *I went over to the chief hospital, which was in excellent*
> *order, and chiefly filled with convalescents. There was*
> *another large establishment, but I could not walk to and*
> *over it, for by this time my feet had become too painful to*
> *allow of further exercise. I shall proceed to see the hos-*
> *pitals for the insane as soon as possible. Meanwhile, I do*
> *not allow my hopes to rise. . . . I see the first difficulty is the*
> *want of persons to execute the trusts of an institution.*
> *But time must show.*

Dorothea realized that putting up a building was only the first
step and that understanding how to help the mentally ill recover was
far more important. When she visited hospitals in Europe and America, she was treated like a queen by the doctors, but always wore
gloves to touch objects and see if the rooms were kept clean. She
would also visit the kitchen, tasting the food to make sure it was

edible. Then she would ask patients, "When was the last time you saw a doctor?"

She was most concerned whether their mental condition was treated. She had created the hospitals and now wanted to find out if they were not just housing the mentally ill but also helping them return to reality.

Nine days later, she wrote Mrs. Rathbone on April 29:

> *I was greatly surprised and much gratified to find in Constantinople a very well directed hospital for the insane in the Turkish quarter, and I failed to discover in either Stamboul or its suburbs any examples of abuse and barbarous usage of this class, so I proceeded to the Greek and Armenian-Christian hospitals, in which, I regret to say, I found very mistaken supervision of all the patients—chains, neglect, and absence of all curative treatment.*
>
> *I think the means I took for the remedy of these abuses will avail to correct them generally in the vicinity of the Turkish Capital, but in the provinces I apprehend that great evils will long exist. . . . The insane of Constantinople are in a* far better condition *than those of Rome or Trieste, and in some respects better cared for than in Turin, Milan, or Ancona. All the patients were Turks, fifty-two men, twenty women, eighteen servants and attendants, three physicians, one resident director, and night watchmen. The hospital was founded by Solyman [sic], the Magnificent, and the provisions for the comfort and pleasure of the patients, including music, quite astonished me. The superintendent proposes improvements. I had* substantially *little to suggest, and* nothing *to urge!!!*

Dr. Cyrus Hamlin, then president of Robert College in Constantinople, sent Tiffany a letter from Lexington, Massachusetts, on August 7, 1889, two years after Dorothea's death, recalling his impressions of her at that time. She had been "a welcome guest" at his house during her visit to Constantinople.

He wrote:

She came and went at pleasure. She had two objects in view, the hospitals and prisons. To these she seemed wholly devoted, although her conversation and her interest, embraced a vast variety of subjects. She often entertained us with the peculiarities of certain officials with whom her work led her to have intercourse.

The most annoying to her were the indifferent. The least annoying were the gruff. She could generally come round that. But the excessively polite she had learned to fear. Her criticisms were always in a kindly spirit, and she clearly saw the humorous as well as the sorrowful in human life.

She visited, I think, all the prisons and hospitals of the great city. These are very numerous, as every nationality, the Armenians, Greeks, Catholic-Armenians, and Turks, has its own. I obtained admission for her to the great Greek hospital of Balloeli, under very favorable circumstances. She was treated very politely. Also in the great Armenian hospital. In both she found departments for the insane, with the management of which she was not pleased. The English prison called forth the severest criticism. Dr. Hayland, who had the medical care, was not pleased with her intrusion. She thought to find it the best, and she pronounced it the worst.

The Turkish debtors' prison she found nauseous for filth and want of ventilation. But she found in the Turkish insane hospital, once one of the horrors of Constantinople, order, cleanliness, light, ventilation, clothing, diet, which left nothing to be desired. Employments also and diversions were equally admirable. She came home at night joyful. She said, "I have found one institution in Constantinople the very best, where I thought to find the very worst."

Dr. Hamlin explained that as a young Turk of wealth and station he had been educated in Paris and while there had become interested in the famous French Hospital for the Insane. He studied the system, was admitted into all sections of the establishment, and was helped to prepare himself for what he felt to be his "mission": to establish the same kind of hospital for his own people.

At Constantinople, Dr. Hamlin said, Dorothea addressed a communication to the heads and managers of the institutions, pointed out what seemed to her desirable changes, and gave them reports and pamphlets that contained useful information. Dr. Hamlin ended his letter: "Miss Dix made the impression at Constantinople of a person of culture, judgment, self-possession, absolute fearlessness in the path of duty, and yet a woman of refinement and true Christian philanthropy. I remember her with the profoundest respect and admiration, and regret that all my correspondence with her is lost."

Dorothea next embarked on a sail up the Danube to Vienna. While her steamer made a landing in Assora, Hungary, she wrote Anne on May 9, 1856:

> *My dear Annie,—Look on your map of Europe, and you may trace my route from Venice, whence I last wrote, to Trieste, Ancona, Molfetta, Brindisi, Corfu, Cephalonia, Zane, Patras, Missolonghi, Mycenae, Corinth, Piraeus, Athens, Syra, Teos, Sangras, Mytilene, Callipoli, Marmora, Constantinople, Bosphorus, Varna, Saluna, mouth of the Danube, Galatz, Balaka, Assora, whence the boat is bound up this grand river to Pesth and Vienna. Why I have made this long route would now occupy too much time to relate, but I hope to meet you face to face, and speak of these and many more subjects.*
>
> *I have the strong hope that I shall not need to return to Rome, for a letter received from my banker there acquainted me that the Pope has listened to my remonstrance and intercession, and restored Dr. Guildini to the charge of the hospital, which augurs well for the residue of my petition, and the fulfillment of the distinct assurances I received before I left Rome. . . .*
>
> *I do not see anything to hinder my embarking for the United States within three months. I am likely to be at Vienna two or three weeks, for the Government has very courteously given me beforehand the entrée of the prisons and the hospitals, and if I do not see much to mend, I may discover something to copy for application at home.*
>
> *I find traveling here alone no more difficult than I should do in any part of America. My usual experience*

attends me. People are civil and obliging, who are treated civilly. . . . I am the sole representative of England and America on the boat. There are, besides, people of many tribes, and persons of far distant English possessions, affording a singular association of oriental costumes and occidental attire. As for speech, Babel is not illy illustrated. . . .

I have resisted the very great temptation of going to Palestine, which I desired more than anything, because I could not afford the expense, though only twelve days distant from Jerusalem. All my life I have wished to visit the Holy City and the sacred places of Syria. As yet, I have confined my journeys to those places where hospitals, or the want of them, have called me. I trust my observations may be applied to some good uses.

She had learned the ship that took her from the United States to England had been lost at sea and wrote, "The impression of the loss of the 'Arctic' is painfully fresh in my recollection. I do not fear at sea, but I never for an hour forget the vicinity or the presence of danger, and, in the event of accident, the almost certain loss of life. *To be ready* is the lesson we should learn, so that if the call be heard on the sea or the land, by day or by night, we may be glad to go home, where our limited capacities may more fully expand, and immortality perfect what time has rightly planted."

After completing her examination of the hospitals of Austria and, in Vienna, urging the promised new asylum in Dalmatia, on the eastern coast of the Adriatic, Dorothea then visited Russia, Sweden, Norway, Denmark, Holland, Belgium, and part of Germany. She finally returned to England by way of France.

She had patiently explored, day by day, the asylums, prisons, and poorhouses of each place she visited, enjoying the moments when she found something to praise and learn from. But whenever she discovered traces of ignorance, neglect, or wrongdoing, she sought to appeal to the highest authorities and to explain the best methods of hospital or prison treatment.

Tiffany pointed out that the strength of the impression produced "by this quiet, sweet-voiced, yet strangely authoritative woman who had come from a land thousands of miles across the sea, and whose unerring eye and immense experience enabled her at a glance to see where to praise and where mercifully to blame, could be judged from a single chance instance that revealed the memory she left behind in Prague, Bohemia."

It remained such a permanent memory that ten years after her return to America she unexpectedly received a large box of highly polished wood, inlaid with the metallic inscription on its top, "To Miss D. L. D. From the American Club of Bohemian Ladies."

The club consisted of "ladies interested in the condition and elevation of the women of Bohemia, or the poorer classes, or wherever a good deed can help a human being." Inside the box lay a brief biography of Dorothea in the Bohemian language; translations of Bohemian poems by Professor Wratislaw, of Christ's College, Cambridge, England; an illustrated quarto of Bohemian National Songs; an album of views of historical interest; and, finally, photographs of distinguished Bohemian women, statesmen, and soldiers, bearing an inscription on ivory: "To Miss D. L. Dix, this album is dedicated as a token of the affection and admiration of the Bohemian Ladies' American Club, Prague, 1808."

Dorothea's arduous journeys and patient explorations brought about changes in most of the countries she visited as she made personal contact with the ablest authorities on insanity. That she was often cheered by as well as depressed at what met her eyes appeared in a note in her handwriting:

"In Russia I saw much to approve and appreciate. As for the issue in the hospitals in St. Petersburg and at Moscow, I really had nothing to ask. Every comfort and all needed care were possessed and much recreation secured,—very little restraint was used. Considering I do not speak the language, I get on wonderfully well, and *see* all that time allows."

She had completed what one of her friends described as a long and detailed "circumnavigation of charity." But to her, it was more than charity, it was necessity. Her life without it would have been unbearable. With it, she could feel needed, engaged in a project that would change the entire attitude of nations toward the indigent insane.

8

New Challenges at Fifty-four

Dorothea set sail from Liverpool to New York aboard the steamship *Baltic* on September 16, 1856. She wrote Anne just before leaving, "I do not fear the sea but I never for an hour forget the vicinity of the presence of danger, and in the event of accident the almost certain loss of life."

She was fifty-four, it had been just two years since she had sought to recuperate abroad from the trying work of her previous fourteen years and the overwhelming defeat of her 12,225,000 Acre Bill, blocked by President Pierce. She had called Pierce a "weak, vacillating executive."

Dr. Tuke, now her good friend, and the venerable Dr. John Conolly, one of the leaders in the history of reducing the plight of the insane, along with Dr. Pinel and Samuel Tuke (Dr. Tuke's father), both told of their feelings for her just before she left.

Dr. Conolly wrote from Hanwell on August 10, one month in advance of her sailing: "My Dear Madam,—Your words of approbation, Dear Miss Dix, are very precious to me; for I honor you and your great labors for the benefit of your fellow-creatures in many ways. . . . God bless you, my dear lady. I trust there are regions where, after this world, all will be more congenial to such spirits, and to those who sympathize with you, and share your good and noble aspirations." He signed it, "Ever faithfully yours."

Two days before she left, Dr. Tuke sent a letter dated September 14 from York: "My dear Friend,—I have pretty much given up the pleasing illusion of seeing you before sailing. . . . I am inclined to envy you the feelings which you must have in the retrospect of what you have been enabled to do since you set foot on British land. I cannot doubt that the day will come when many, very many, will rise up to call you Blessed. Blessed to them, who, until they have been relieved from their bodily infirmities, cannot thank you for what you have done, and the yet more you have longed to be able to do for them." He signed it, "Your truly attached friend, Daniel H. Tuke."

Dorothea's voyage home was smooth and sunny. Near the end, she wrote the Rathbones: "We are still getting on well, and already land birds come to the vessel for food and rest. They are very familiar and eat from our hands. One flew into the open window near me while at dinner to-day, rested on the table by the captain's plate, picked up some crumbs, and, finally satisfied, flew away,—perhaps for the distant land, fifty miles off."

Appeals for renewed work from various quarters of the United States and Canada awaited Dorothea. They emphasized the need for new hospitals, fresh extensions, large appropriations. It had been the hope of many old friends that she would now devote herself to writing a book in which she would explain the results of her immense range of observations in Europe.

As Tiffany said, the habits of a lifetime were not to be altered; she could not be expected to take time to write a book. She needed to act on what she had seen and learned abroad that applied to her country's needs, rather than sit down quietly to describe her contributions to mankind. All her life Dorothea refused to place herself in the limelight, anathema to her.

She wrote Anne from New York on December 26 that she was back at work. She had "spent Tuesday at Ward's, Randall's and Blackwell's Islands," in New York; on Wednesday, she had gone "up the Hudson to Sing Sing prison and on Thursday, to High Bridge, to see juvenile asylums and reformatories; tomorrow she would go to Bloomingdale's, another asylum. On Saturday she would visit more hospitals, then spend Saturday evening at the New Jersey State Hospital as it was now called, in Trenton, a mammoth institution spreading over many acres, her "first child."

She added in her letter to Anne, "Wednesday I set out for Buffalo, Geneva, Canandaigua, etc., to explain anew the miseries of almshouses so if you do not hear from me, please do not consider yourself forgotten nor even unbeloved." She also said she was recommending special training for "idiots and feeble-minded children," up to now completely ignored.

For her, the founding of the many asylums she fondly called her "children," bore almost the same relation to the work demanded for their extension and full development as did the bringing up of a child. It was a Herculean feat to carry a bill for the establishment of a new asylum for the indigent insane through a state legislature. But this was only the first step. To get the institution well manned, to help cures become affective and chronic misery relieved, and to gain friends for what society believed were unsavory places brought out anxieties that Dorothea now lived with day after day and long into the night.

Over the years, many appreciated her quiet but effective work. When she was seventy-one, Dr. J. M. Cleaveland of the Hudson River State Hospital in New York, wrote: "Your devotion to duty in starting off in that pitiless Monday's storm touched all our hearts. The lesson it inculcated was more than a chapter of moral maxims, and I hope we may never forget it."

In five years the Civil War would break out, and Dorothea would turn her energies temporarily in a new direction. But until 1861, she worked hard to raise even larger appropriations of money for the existing mental hospitals. These were the years of the enlargement of nearly all the asylums she founded, as well as the starting of a number of new ones.

She also helped enhance the understanding of the importance of caring, thoughtful personnel in the asylums. She early became aware that the personal feelings of a superintendent and his physicians were often that of men who felt the patient was like a powder magazine that might explode at any minute. The caretakers feared the "crazies," rather than wished to help them recover.

Outside also lay a fearful public with strong suspicions of what went on inside the hospital where dangerous madmen were cooped up, probably until they died or killed each other. The public visualized cunning, deceitful, mentally sick men and women as the prey of wild hallucinations and often suffering a degraded sexual passion, unable to tell the difference between fantasy and fact. A patient's account of being brutalized by others was often fantasy, though, at times, unfortunately true.

The management of hospitals appealed to Dorothea as part of her clear judgment and sympathy for the insane. She believed strongly that her recommendation of someone for a high post at a mental hospital should be kept secret. This belief was so strong that when Dr. John W. Ward of Trenton learned from his trustees, some years after his appointment as superintendent, that he owed it to the emphatic recommendation of Dorothea and he graciously thanked her, she turned on him sharply. She denounced the revelation as a betrayal of confidence that others had permitted him to know it.

Dorothea started a letter in Cleveland to Mrs. Rathbone on July 21, 1857. A new hospital was to be founded near Pittsburgh on the plan of the Rauhe Haus in Hamburg, Germany, and the community was asked to contribute to the prospective hospital. Dorothea wrote: "I am here in Cleveland only for a few days, and proceed to Zelienople, and thence to Pittsburgh, where I hope to complete what I have begun and advanced there. I have induced the managers of the proposed benevolent Institution to sell the farm which had been purchased, and which is not well situated, and take a magnificent location for a hospital on a fine elevated site which I found on the Ohio River, eight miles from Pittsburgh, and which is both salubrious and cheerful, joined with outlooks of rare beauty associated with some elements of grandeur."

She did not finish the letter until August 10 when in Zelienople, Pennsylvania:

> *I was broken off from my writing more than a fortnight*
> *since. Here at Zelienople, I am both looking for a farm well*
> *situated and well watered, and studying an Institution*

*having chiefly the features of the celebrated Rauhe Haus
at Horn near Hamburg. It is a new Reformator erected by
a noble-minded clergyman of the German Lutheran
persuasion,—one of those men of rare power, Fénelon-like
spirit, and Apostolic self-sacrifice whom we occasionally
see rising up to show the astonished world how much one
man can do through the force of moral power without
riches save the riches of a sanctified spirit. . . .*

*I proceed to-morrow to Economy, hoping to secure
from the followers of that singular man Rapp, the Sua-
bian [sic] peasant who emigrated with his family to the
United States more than fifty years ago, a contribution
for hospital uses. The large wealth accumulated by singular skill and industry, before the death of their leader
and founder, Rapp, is stored in secret, and no doubt
before many years will escheat to the Commonwealth.
They have no longer hopes or expectations. The prophetic
declarations of their Founder are falsified, and now a
handful remain where once their name was "Legion."
One seeks of them charities as conferring on their stag-
nant life a real benefit. Lately they gave $500 to the new
hospital.*

The year 1858 began with a letter to Mrs. Rathbone on January 25,
reporting from Oneida, New York:

*Snow two feet deep, thermometer 27 degrees below zero,
gas-burners easily light by the spark transmitted by the
finger. Thus it is not difficult to realize the severity of the
cold so often described by Arctic voyagers. Do you hear
anything of Mrs. Chisholm, that woman of transcendent
worth? I have often wished I could do something that
would show her how much good hearts in this Western
world appreciate her and her works. How is Miss Carpen-
ter succeeding? I have great faith that the school and
discipline on the Ackbar will finally succeed. Our work of
Reform seems gigantic, and most discouraging if the
whole field is taken at once; but if each does his or her
part, we may hope for final success.*

She signed the letter, "Your steadfast friend, D. L. Dix."

She lost a dear friend, the Reverend Samuel Gilman, the Unitarian minister of Charleston, South Carolina, a man of such sanctity of spirit that his funeral services were attended by Catholic priests, Jewish rabbis, Episcopalian rectors and Baptist, Methodist, and Presbyterian ministers. A few years before his death, Dr. Gilman paid Dorothea two lines of reverential tribute:

> *To D. L. D.*
> *One pain alone thy visit gives—our shame*
> *To live so far beneath thy own great aim.*

Dorothea spent the earlier part of the year in Texas, trying to avoid the cold weather. In that chiefly unvisited section of the Union, she had expected to find herself a stranger and felt delighted at the cordiality of her reception.

The first of her letters to intimate friends in colder states appeared on March 28, 1859, when she wrote Mrs. Hare in Philadelphia from Austin, Texas. In that letter, she gave an account of how she accompanied a number of the poor insane to a hospital:

> *You ask, perhaps how I occupied myself under these adverse circumstances as poor, sick, insane people were transported such distances over such roads! I am thankful that I came, because I find much to do, and people take me by the hand as a beloved friend.*
>
> *My eyes fill with tears at the hourly heartwarm welcome; the confidence, the cordial good-will, and the successions of incidents, proving that I do in very truth dwell in the hearts of my countrymen. I am so astonished that my wishes in regard to Institutions, my opinions touching organization, are considered definitive. A gentleman in the State Service said to me, "You are a moral autocrat; you speak and your word is law." People say, "O, you are no stranger. We have known you years and years."*

Mrs. Samuel Torrey wrote in a letter to her: "I have been desired by Mr. Gannett to inform you that a man called upon him a few days ago, and put into his hands $100 for you from the mother of a shipwrecked seaman who had been saved by one of your life-boats when wrecked off the coast of Newfoundland. Mr. Gannett questioned the man, but could not elicit any information respecting the woman. The money was to be employed to assist poor seamen."

She replied to Mrs. Torrey's letter, from Baton Rouge, Louisiana, on April 7:

> *My Dear Friend,—Mr. Torrey can hold the $100 on interest till I can find leisure to apply it advantageously. I shall be glad to increase its amount a little by adding something to it myself. I can build another lifeboat which I want. . . . I have been needing lifeboats myself in the Gulf of Mexico last month. We just escaped foundering. In fact, for twenty-four hours the captain did not leave his station on the deck. . . .*
>
> *In Texas everybody was kind, obliging, and most attentive. I had a hundred instances that filled my eyes with tears. I did not imagine anybody would know me there, but on the contrary, I was claimed and acknowledged as a dear friend in such wise as has made a lasting impression on my heart and mind. I was taking a dinner at a small public house on a wide, lonely prairie. The master stood, with the stage way-bill in his hand, eyeing me, I thought, because I was the only lady passenger, but when I drew out my purse to pay as usual, his quick expression was, "No, no, by George! I don't take money from you; why, I never thought I should see you, and now you are in my house! You have done good to everybody for years and years. Make sure now there's a home for you in every house in Texas. Here, wife, this is Miss Dix! Shake hands, and call the children."*
>
> *Don't think me conceited in relating this incident. It is one of a hundred in Texas, one of a thousand this winter all through the South. I am constantly surprised by spontaneous expressions of the heartiest good-will, and I may well be careful what I demand for hospitals, etc., for my work is unquestioned, and so I try to be very prudent and watchful.*

A letter she sent to Anne on December 8, 1859, from Columbia, South Carolina, bears witness to the same enthusiastic gratitude from others in another state:

> *I arrived here Saturday greeted and welcomed on all sides by private friends and public authorities. I have really been quite astonished at the public expressions of welcome. I am very happy in knowing I am much beloved by my fellow-citizens in this part of the Union. "We will prove our regard for you by our acts in behalf of those for whom you plead," said a Senator who spoke as the representative of the body. I could not measure half the pleasant words uttered. "Our State will always welcome you as to a home, and so will we at our firesides among the wives and children." "Yes! yes! that we will," sounded forth spontaneously from all who were present.*

She ended the letter, "I have sent you egotistical lines, Annie; keep them to yourself." She knew Anne would understand, from the start there had been a lasting love and friendship between them, each wanting the best for the other.

Tiffany comments that it was "a matter for congratulation" that Anne placed all Dorothea's letters in a safe place from which one day they would appear in his book. We have him to thank for the full picture that has emerged of Dorothea's life and work.

After a hearty reception for her in the hall of the South Carolina House of Representatives, Dorothea wrote Anne from New Orleans: "I have traveled the past thirty-two days and nights, and this of necessity, so that I lie down now and sleep any hour I can, to make up lost time, and to-day I am feeling a good deal refreshed. I am bound from this place to Baton Rouge, and thence by land to Jackson, La., next to Bayou Sara, to Vicksburg by river, thence by railroad to Jackson, Miss., after that to Memphis, thence to St. Louis, thence up the Missouri to the State Hospital at Fulton, returning to Jacksonville, Ill., and to Springfield."

In another note to Anne from Jackson, Mississippi, Dorothea reported, "So far as I can see a favorable impression is made, and there is a probability that I shall get an appropriation of $80,000. I ask this winter in different States more than a third of a million."

Her recent life had been spent in traveling, first throughout Europe, then across America. She had no home of her own, just as she often felt as a little girl when sent to spend time at her grandparents. She never felt completely at home when she moved into Dix Mansion for two years and then was sent to her great-aunt's home in Worcester for almost four years before returning to Boston and setting up her two schools.

The railroad "sleeping car" was now introduced to American travelers. Dorothea's first feeling was one of hatred. She wrote Anne from Jackson, Mississippi: "I *saw* some sleeping cars. That was enough. Nothing would induce me to occupy one of them, they are quite *detestable*. I did make one night's experiment later, between Pittsburgh and Cincinnati: that will suffice for the rest of life. I cannot suppose that persons of decent habits, especially ladies, will occupy them, unless some essential changes are made in their arrangements and regulations."

She felt that for women there was no privacy. Women had to undress and sleep in the company of men. Dorothea, except in the case of her one mission in life, was very shy.

According to Tiffany, a letter at the end of 1859, for her a fruitful year, "contains the fullest detailed description she left behind of any of her brilliant dashes of energy and courage. Written in a vein of humorous enjoyment of the scene, it unconsciously furnishes a striking exhibition of that lightning-swift dispatch with which—however overweighted with other cares, she stood ready to turn instantly aside to right a wrong appearing from any new quarter."

The letter was sent to Mrs. Rathbone in England. Several New York papers had given highly sensational accounts of the attack of a "rescuing party" in New York State led by Dorothea. Her letter started:

Did I write you an account of my affair with, or in connection to, some kidnapped Indians? While in Albany, in the State Library last month, several persons being with me consulting on pending questions, a white man and an

*Indian entered, and the former said, "There is Miss Dix;
come, tell her your story!" It was this: Near Syracuse, in
Central New York, is an Indian settlement of five hundred
souls. A company of circus riders and strolling players,
visiting Syracuse, thought it might be a good speculation
to entice some of the Indians from this village to New
York, three hundred miles distant, embark with them for
Europe, and make a show of the Aborigines for their own
profit.*

*To this end they proceeded to the Indian village, selected
their dupes,—six lads of about fourteen, and several
squaws, with one or two infants. Promising them fine
shows and sights in Syracuse, they induced them to go
there. This excited no other attention than a little feeling of
envy amongst those who could not witness the promised
exhibitions. After the plays were over, the above-named
Indians were persuaded to get on a night train of cars and
"take a little ride." This little ride ended only in the city of
New York, and still held by blinding promises they were
taken to a remote tavern on the outskirts of the city, and
there strictly watched till the vessel was ready in which the
company designed to embark.*

*Meanwhile, one of the boys managed to escape and
found his way to his own people, reporting the captivity of
his companions. The father of two of the boys, a chief,
hastened to the city, but the journey consumed his little
stock of money, and, however bold and at home in the
forests, the mighty city of New York, and the people with
whose language he was so little familiar thronging everywhere, yet unheeding his perplexities, made him fearful
and troubled.*

*He came up the river again as far as Albany, saw a man
on the street he knew, and related his troubles. This man, a
doorkeeper at the State Capitol, brought him to me, and
after a few minutes' consideration, I, taking with me the
Indian, proceeded to the office of the Regent of the University and asked the professor to attend me to the Executive
Chambers.*

They were crowded, but the Governor was my friend

and my host, for I was at that time a guest at Government House. At once I stated the case, asking authority to send to the city for the release of the captive Indians. The State attorney was sent for, but not being particularly prompt, nor giving in the sequence any very lucid opinion, I turned away. The Governor gave the Indian sufficient money to pay his expenses back by car to New York, one hundred and thirty miles.

I took leave, and sent a page to the Senate Chamber for one of the city Senators. That body was specially engaged. I repeated my message urgently, and Mr. Spencer came. I stated the case. He wrote an order to the Chief of Police, directing him to make search for the missing parties and deliver them to the chief, and by all means prevent their embarkation.

I then addressed a letter to the District Attorney of New York, and now it wanted but ten minutes to the departure of the cars south. I bade the Indian run to the station,—an Indian can always run,—giving him the sealed packages, and to say, on arriving in the city, to the conductor of the train that he wanted a policeman to guide him to the captain's office—being there to deliver the papers and wait the result.

It appears all went well thus far. The Chief of Police detailed a party of policemen, and the "Show Company" were found occupying a low tavern in the suburbs, and concealed in a back room where they watched their Onandaga [sic] captives. The five boys were immediately taken, though some opposition and a show of fight were made. The next day a second party went out to take the remainder of the Indians, and now thirty or forty partisans of the company, rowdies of the baser sort, being collected, a fight commenced. The police were assailed with stones, knives, and blows, but eventually carried their point, besides arresting some of the leaders of the affray and the landlord.

The Indians were all conveyed to the North River Station, free passage given to Albany, and dispatched to the Seat of Government with a letter to Governor King, and the next day some news-scavenger threw into the columns

*of a newspaper a history of the affair with embellishments
and—using my name as chief patroness of all people in
adversity or otherwise oppressed,—so oddly mixed up the
story as to make it look very much as if I were not content
with the more quiet part of the performance, but had
heroically led the attack, not by pen, but by armed force.*

*I send this hastily written letter off without looking to
see what is so carelessly put together. I invite myself to be
your guest five years from now, all of us surviving that
period, and I trust you will live many long and good years.*

God bless you and yours. Truly yours, D. L. Dix.

There now remained a little over a year before the outbreak of the
Civil War. The war was to end temporarily Dorothea's work in the
mental health area as she helped a completely different cause. She
would give up for four years her work with the mentally ill to help
save the North from annihilation at the hands of the South, which
wanted to keep the blacks their prisoners.

9

THE WAR AT HOME EXPLODES

The seeds of the Civil War grew larger as several states threatened to secede from the Union. In spite of this threat, Dorothea wrote her constant, across-the-seas friend Mrs. Rathbone on March 18, 1860, from Harrisburg, Pennsylvania, that she hoped to see her soon and thanked her once again for taking care of her when she had felt so incapacitated. She knew the Rathbones admired her work, since they wrote constantly to learn of her latest projects.

In the letter she said that the idea of visiting the Rathbones

will not give way even when I see how much one can find to do, even laboring with constant diligence. Should I *recross the ocean, I should greatly desire to do something for the* Private Houses, *hospitals they cannot be called, for the hapless insane, whose greatest calamity is in being cast within their imprisoning walls.*

This horror haunts me like an ill dream, or a fearful remembrance of what it is actually, a series of most

dreadful facts, *I cannot excuse or forgive the English
Commissioners of Lunacy. They surely should know their
duty, if they do not; but their dull eyes and sluggish, far-
separated visitations have revealed something of the
dreary horrors of those beaten receptacles sustained by a
Christian people.*

*They are too indolent to exert the influence their official
station gives to remedy, at least in a measure, what their
criminal sufferance makes them participants in maintaining. If I could have* authority, *I would not let one
circling moon pass her changes, before I was again upon
that field of toil—and neither time nor thought should be
spared in the service. But I must turn from this subject, on
which I never allow myself to think at all, if I can help it.*

She again wrote Mrs. Rathbone from Prairie du Chien, Wiscon-
sin, on her way to Minnesota on August 27, explaining she was
writing at a side table in a telegraph office, waiting for a boat to La
Crosse, after which "I shall push up the Mississippi, Fort Snelling,
and St. Anthony."

She thanked Mrs. Rathbone for her "so pleasant and refreshing"
letters that often cheered her up. She continued: "I expect to be in
the Northwest, in this wonderful country of vast prairies, with deep,
ocean-reaching rivers, and lakes that deceive you into the idea that
you are where the Atlantic rushes in upon the resisting shores of the
Eastern States."

She noted,

*The country is packed with luckless foreigners. Well, the
world at present is large enough for all. If all would do
their part for the general good, how would the earth become as "the Garden of the Lord." The German and the
Norwegian element is making a mark here, and their people in the main are industrious, saving, and orderly, except a remnant of the former who are in life and character
very coarse and brutal, and singularly addicted to wife-
tyranny,—beating and often killing the poor drudges of
the household. The insane of this class of Germans and of
the South of Ireland people are rarely cured, and so they go*

*to swell the amount of those who crowd the incurable
wards of hospitals.*

A third letter to Mrs. Rathbone was sent from Columbia, South
Carolina, on December 19, 1860. In it, she explained, "I made a
rapid journey hither by railroad from Jackson, Miss., traveling to
Washington without stopping a half hour three days and three
nights, and arriving to find all hospital business not at a standstill
merely, but looking very unpromising. I had no time to lose, and at
once saw the Senate and House Committees, reasoned, explained,
persuaded, urged, till I secure a unanimous report from these parties to their respective bodies in favor of an extension by new wings,
etc., of the State Hospital for the Insane. Thus the work is fairly
commended."

Her bill passed both Senate and House by an almost unanimous
vote. It provided $60,000 for support of the asylum toward the
foundation of which she had worked from 1852 to 1858. The same
winter she carried through a bill in Tennessee for a new hospital in
Knoxville and raised a large appropriation for one she had founded in
Nashville. These amounts, along with $100,000 obtained in Pennsyl-
vania, represented only a portion of her work during 1860.

She wrote Anne from Frankfort, Kentucky, in March 1861, that
"all my Bills have passed. My winter has been fully successful. I have
had great cares, greater fatigues, many dangers, countless blessings
unmeasured, preserving mercies, and am joined to all occasions for
thanksgiving—well, and still able to work very satisfactorily. . . .
God spare our distressed country."

She believed the election to the presidency of Abraham Lincoln
would lead to war with the South. For years she had been in close
personal contact with the leaders of public opinion in the South, so
she understood how they felt. Knowing if she uttered one word on
the slavery question she would destroy her ability to do anything
further for the indigent insane, she had kept silent on the issue as
she engaged in her usual work.

She wrote Anne in spring 1861, "I thank God, dear Annie, I have
such full uses for time now, for the state of our beloved country,
otherwise, would crush my heart and life. I was never so unhappy
but once before, and that grief was more selfish perhaps, viz., when

the 12,225,000 Acre Bill was killed by a poor, base man in power," referring to President Pierce.

In April 1861 President Lincoln called for 75,000 volunteer troops to defend Washington. Massachusetts was the first to respond, with two regiments, the Sixth and the Eighth. The next morning the secessionists in Baltimore retaliated by burning the railroad bridges between Washington and Philadelphia, cutting off communication between Washington and the Northern states.

The president of the Philadelphia and Baltimore Railroad, Samuel M. Felton, instantly seized the Southern steamboats on the river, and the arrival on the following day of the second contingent of the Massachusetts troops under General Benjamin F. Butler saved Washington.

According to Felton, Dorothea played an important part in the preparations taken to meet this critical juncture. He wrote that he "again and again besought Miss Dix to permit him to make known how much the country owed her, but that she had always given a point-blank refusal to have any use made of her name." Seven years later he wrote Tiffany, describing his recollections of Dorothea, showing the part she took in saving Washington:

> *Early in the year 1861, Miss Dix, the Philanthropist, came into my office on a Saturday afternoon. I had known her for some years as one engaged in alleviating the sufferings of the afflicted. Her occupation in building hospitals had brought her into contact with prominent men in the South. She had become familiar with the structure of Southern society, and also with the working of its political machinery. She stated to me that she had an important communication to make to me personally.*
>
> *I listened attentively to what she had to say for more than an hour. She put in a tangible and reliable shape by the facts she related what before I had heard in numerous and detached parcels. The sum of it all was, that there was then an extensive and organized conspiracy through the South to seize upon Washington, with its archives and records, and then declare the Southern Confederacy de facto the Government of the United States.*

> *At the same time they were to cut off all means of communication between Washington and the North, East, and West, and thus prevent the transportation of troops to wrest the Capital from the hands of the insurgents. Mr. Lincoln's inauguration was thus to be prevented, or his life was to fall a sacrifice. In fact, she said, troops were then drilling on the line of our own road, the Washington and Annapolis line, and other lines of railroad. The men drilled were to obey the commands of their leaders, and the leaders were banded together to capture Washington.*

Felton was so impressed by this interview that he told the leaders in Washington the full extent of the peril as Dorothea outlined it. Detectives were hired to enlist as volunteers in the various squads of Southerners who were secretly drilling along the lines of railroad from Harrisburg and Philadelphia to Baltimore and Washington. They learned of the enemy's plans, including its intention to assassinate Abraham Lincoln on his way to the Capitol to be inaugurated president.

The Northern leaders immediately sent troops to the area and captured the Southern would-be murderers. Felton thus averted this drastic danger and secretly smuggled the president-elect through to Washington. But Dorothea had been the one to alert the country's leaders to these perils, which, in all probability, helped preserve not only Lincoln's life but the survival of Washington. She never met President Lincoln, but she would serve him well.

Three hours following the massacre of the Southerners in Baltimore, she reached that city in the midst of the tumult and made her way through the crowded streets. She boarded the last train permitted to leave for Washington. She was on her way to answer the call for volunteers—to report for nursing duties—now needed by her country for a different kind of work.

As she wrote Anne from Washington on April 20, 1861: "Yesterday I followed in the train three hours after the tumult in Baltimore. It was not easy getting across the city, but I did not choose to turn back, and so I reached my place of destination. I think my duty lies near military hospitals for the present. This need not be announced. I have reported myself and some nurses for free service at the War Department and to the Supreme General."

Dorothea received the first commission of its kind ever issued to a woman when she was appointed superintendent of the United States Army nurses on June 10, 1861. One of her most valuable nurses would be Louisa May Alcott, author of *Little Women* and other books, who rushed south from her home in Boston to offer her services.

Dorothea's job was to select and assign women nurses to general or permanent military hospitals, "they *not* to be employed in such a hospital without her sanction and approval, except in cases of urgent need." Orders were issued by Simon Cameron, secretary of war, and D. C. Wood, acting surgeon general.

Her work applied to the women nurses of the military hospitals, which was different from Florence Nightingale's serving on the field of battle, easing the pain of severely wounded soldiers. The North expected that within a few months the war would end. Instead, four years of deadly struggle would ensue, more than a million men arrayed on each side. The North would eventually need not a single woman, nearly sixty years old and at times in ill health, but large organized groups at twenty different nursing centers.

An army of efficient subordinates, run by able administrative minds, now arose to deal with the powerful organizations that had large sums of money at their disposal. They built storehouses at a hundred different points and established trains of army wagons in the field and departmental divisions with experts to run them. Women nurses volunteered by the thousands, the majority without the knowledge to fit them for backbreaking experiences they never dreamed of.

Dorothea rented one house at 500 Twelfth Street and a second on H Street. In the first she set up temporary headquarters for nurses; in the second, she organized a canteen for soldiers. Volunteers soon arrived in cattle cars and stood in long lines on the streets under hot and drenching rain, sometimes for eighteen hours, as the quarter-masters sought a place to feed and shelter them. Some died in the streets from typhoid, dysentery, and measles of a virulent type that began to sweep the army. Dorothea found an old hotel in Georgetown, tore out the dingy carpets, scrubbed the walls, filled clean tickings with straw, commandeered cots, and took in sick volunteers.

When the Union Army was defeated at Bull Run, the men reeled back to Washington in bloody bandages, sometimes dragging wounded comrades, as the stench of death filled the streets.

Dorothea bought fresh vegetables, fruits and preserves and also appealed for linens, lint, and bedclothes for the wounded. She rushed to Alexandria near the scene of battle, saw the wounded lying in pools of mud, reddened with their own blood, bought an ambulance, and brought the men back to Washington to be tended by her nurses. She worked night and day with her volunteers to sort the boxes of lint, bandages, and medicines that rolled in from all over the nation at her request.

The surgeon general ruled that women could not serve on the battlefields, only at base hospitals now hastily set up in and near Washington. But when, from Harrison's Landing, a desperate assistant surgeon wired, "Send thirty nurses at once," Dorothea led them there, setting up a base hospital when she found blood and disorder everywhere.

She wrote Mrs. Rathbone, after a young soldier clung to her hand as he lay dying, "This war in my own country is breaking my heart."

She found herself taking care of Louisa May Alcott, who had fallen ill with pneumonia, at the Georgetown hospital. Miss Alcott later wrote of Dorothea, "Daily our Florence Nightingale climbed the steep stairs stealing a moment from her busy life to watch over the stranger of whom she was thoughtfully tender as any mother. Long may she wave." Another time Miss Alcott wrote, "Whatever others may think or say of Miss Dix, this nurse is forever grateful for the tokens which appeared by her pillow, none of them more valuable than the D. D. written on the flyleaf of that precious Bible, initials which mean more to me than Doctor of Divinity."

Though not a nurse herself, and without hospital experience, Dorothea had profited from her many years of observing how hospitals functioned. She had been unofficial adviser to many hospitals, visited military hospitals abroad, and become acquainted with hospital organizations. If she found a doctor who was intoxicated while on duty, she reported him at once to the surgeon general and he would be dishonorably discharged. She had nearly 180 nurses to control. She also walked through the wards handing out books, fruit, and flowers from a basket she carried on her arm. On March 16, 1863, she wrote to Anne: "As yet I have not been off duty for a day since the rebellion. I trust I have both grace and strength to carry forward my work till the end."

Dorothea did not feel well as her body became sapped with malaria, overwork, and pulmonary weakness. For years she had been a lonely, single-handed worker, planning her own projects. She now tried to fulfill all the demands made on her, but often became involved in arguments with leading medical officials and regimental surgeons. Her aims for the care of the sick and wounded soldiers were high. She finally exclaimed, "This is not the work I would have my life judged by!" Tiffany reported.

But she fought the battle gamely. Through the four long years, she never took a day's furlough. She remained at her post, organizing bands of nurses, forwarding supplies, and inspecting hospitals. She relieved a heroic amount of suffering and saved many lives. Testimony to her work appeared in a letter from Dr. Carline A. Burghardt, who served the sick and the wounded:

> She was a very retiring, sensitive woman, yet brave and bold as a lion to do battle for the right and for justice. She was very unpopular in the war with surgeons, nurses, and any others, who failed to do their whole duty, and they disliked to see her appear, as she was sure to do if needed. . . . She was one who found no time to make herself famous with pen and paper, but a hard, earnest worker, living in the most severely simple manner, often having to be reminded that she needed food.
>
> To those of us who were privileged to know her, her memory is, and ever will be, very dear. Every day recalls some of her noble acts of kindness and self-sacrifice to mind. She seemed to me to lead a dual life, one for the outside world, the other for her trusted, tried friends.

The new secretary of war, Edwin M. Stanton, believed in her wholeheartedly. So high was his sense of the country's indebtedness to the woman who had first warned Washington of the imminent danger of the Southern attack and who was the last to quit her post of duty, that at the close of war he appealed to her to learn in what shape it would be most agreeable to have her services officially recognized. A public meeting presided over by the highest officials or a grant of money from Congress had been proposed.

Dorothea declined both. When asked what honor she would like, she replied, "The Flags of my Country." A large pair of the national flags were made for her, and the War Department issued the following on December 3, 1866, headed, *"Order in Relation to the Services of Miss Dix"*: "In token and acknowledgment of the inestimable services rendered by Miss Dorothea L. Dix for the Care, Succor, and Relief of the Sick and Wounded Soldiers of the United States on the Battle-Field, in Camps and Hospitals during the recent War, and of her benevolent and diligent labors and devoted efforts to whatever might contribute to their comfort and welfare, it is ordered that a Stand of Arms of the United States National Colors be presented to Miss Dix." It was signed by "Edwin M. Stanton, Secretary of War."

The execution of the order was communicated on January 14, 1867, by General E. D. Townsend, of the War Department's Adjutant General's office, as he wrote Dorothea at No. 2 Pearl Street, Boston, Massachusetts: "My Dear Miss Dix,—I have the pleasure of sending by express this day, in obedience to an order of Mr. Stanton, Secretary of War, a box containing a Stand of the United States Colors presented to you by the Secretary. I trust they will arrive safely. With great respect, your obedient servant, E. D. Townsend."

Dorothea replied to both General Townsend and General Stanton. She wrote Townsend from Albany, New York, on January 25, 1867: "Dear Sir,—I am just in receipt of your letter of the 14th, and acknowledge with the deep emotion of a patriotic heart, my sense of the honor conferred by the presentation through you from the Secretary of War of a Stand of the United States Colors. No greater distinction could have been conferred on me, and the value of this gift is greatly enhanced by the quiet manner in which it is bestowed. Respectfully, D. L. Dix."

To "Honorable Edwin M. Stanton" she wrote that same day: "Sir,—I beg to express my sense of the honorable distinction conferred on me by the Secretary of War, in the presentation of a Stand

134 HEART'S WORK

of United States Colors received by order through Assistant Adjutant General Townsend. No more precious gift could have been bestowed, and no possession will be so prized while life remains to love and serve my country. Very respectfully and with well-grounded esteem, D. L. Dix."

She later bequeathed the flags to Harvard College, where they hang today in the Memorial Hall dedicated to the Sons of Harvard who died for their country in the war for the maintenance of the Union.

When the war finally ended, Dorothea remained in Washington for a while, comforting sick soldiers and the wives and mothers who came hunting for the missing who had not been reported as dead or alive. She carried on a large correspondence with those who sought their loved ones, according to Baker.

In her duties as superintendent of the United States Army Nurses, she had seen a large number of soldiers dying in hospitals under her charge. Also, for hundreds who had been wounded but recovered, as well as numerous nurses who were invalided in their work, left poor and unprovided for, she undertook the role of volunteer pension agent. This task meant hard work for eighteen months to follow. Her services to a large number of the poor and uninfluential were made valuable by her authority with the War Department.

She wished to erect an enduring monument to the memory of the thousands of brave fighters who lay in the newly established National Cemetery at Hampton, Virginia, near Fortress Monroe. The idea of such a monument had been conceived by others, who decided they would transfer the burden to her. She gladly took over; it seemed to her disloyal and outrageous that such a memorial should not be erected.

Her first mention of any personal connection with this project was in a letter to Mrs. Rathbone, written from Washington, D.C., on August 18, 1866:

> Lately I have collected in a quiet way among my friends $8,000 with which to erect a granite monument at Fortress Monroe where are interred more than 6,000 of our brave, loyal soldiers. . . . I had especial direction over most of these martyred to a sacred cause, and never forget the

*countless last messages of hundreds of dying men to fa-
thers, mothers, wives, and children; never forget the calm,
manly fortitude which sustained them through the an-
guish of mortal wounds and the agonies of dissolution.*

*Nothing, in a review of the past four years' war, so
astonishes me as the uniformly calm and firm bearing of
these soldiers of a good cause, dying without a murmur as
they had suffered without a complaint. Thank Heaven the
war is over. I would that its memories also could pass
away.*

She spent weeks visiting quarry after quarry along the coast of
Maine, trying to find granite of such imperishable quality that it
would symbolize the character of the men it honored. When the
structure was completed, she said: "It promises to stand for centuries unless an earthquake should shake it down."

By December 11, 1867, she could write Mrs. Torrey: "Reaching
Washington, I proceeded at once to the Ordnance Bureau to see
Major General Dyer, wrote a letter to General Grant, which was
signed 'approved' by General Dyer, asking for 1,000 muskets and
bayonets, 15 rifled guns and a quantity of 24-pound shot, with which
to construct my fence. I am rather gratified that every bill has been
paid as soon as forwarded."

The completed monument was handed over to the care of the
United States Government early in May 1868. On May 12, she
received a letter from Secretary Stanton, of the "War Department,
Washington City," saying: "Dear Madam,—Inasmuch as by the Act
of Congress the National Cemeteries are placed in charge of the
Secretary of War, and under his direction, I accept with pleasure the
tender of this memorial to our gallant dead, and return the thanks of
the Department to the public-spirited citizens who have furnished
the means for erecting it; and to yourself for your arduous, patriotic,
humane and benevolent labors in bringing to a successful completion such a noble testimonial to our gallant dead who perished in the
war to maintain their government and suppress the rebellion."

Dorothea had continued her lifelong trait of refusing to accept
credit or reward for her work because she insisted it should go to
those she felt deserved it far more.

Her old friend, Dr. Isaac Ray, when he heard of her work on the Monument, wrote: "I congratulate you on the completion of your Monument. With so much stone and iron on your shoulders, I do not wonder you got sick. Pray, do take a lighter load the next time you undertake to shoulder other people's burdens."

The monument Dorothea chose was an obelisk of syenite rising seventy-five feet and resting on a massive base twenty-seven feet square. It was enclosed by a circular fence of the musket barrels, bayonets, and rifled cannon she had selected to be set in heavy blocks of stone.

It contains the simple inscription, "In Memory of Union Soldiers who Died to maintain the Laws." The soldiers were heroic in one way, Dorothea was heroic in another. She honored them as she honored the poor insane she wished to keep from dying prematurely as they fought inner battles they could not conquer alone. Battles that, if faced in time with the help of wise physicians, would often lead to a renewed life of sanity.

10
RETURN TO HER HEART'S WORK

Still active at sixty-five, weighing only ninety-five pounds, and wishing to continue the work she would pursue until she was eighty, Dorothea returned to her lifelong passion of helping those who had lost their reason because of inner terrors.

She received many letters from those awaiting her return. One came from Alfred Huger, of Charleston, South Carolina, showing how thankful people, even the enemy, were that she was once more available for the mentally ill. He wrote:

> It is the instinct of the afflicted to be aroused and encouraged when your name is mentioned. Ruin and desolation hold their court among us. Our poor little State is sinking under a weight of calamity and of woe, our tempers are draped in mourning, and our hearts are in the dust. Still, we flock to the altar when the High Priestess is there.
>
> I was one of the founders of the lunatic asylum. Everywhere and at all times I watched its progress. During the

war I was in daily, almost hourly, interchange with our valued friend, Dr. Parker, and with that household of wounded minds over which he presides, and, as we believe, doing so with a holy purpose. Dr. Parker is the father, brother, and friend, the very "shield and buckler" of our stricken brethren.

We have heard, like a summons to meet death, of his possible removable, and we have heard also of your providential advent. If the authorities that rule over us select this man as a victim, or if Dr. Parker himself can endure his surroundings no longer, then there is an agony upon us, and may we not appeal to you for succor and help? We must not look in vain, and we will not look in vain! Dr. Parker has no equal in our State for the position he occupies. You have no superior, with your mission signed in the High Chancery of Heaven, and witnessed by angels who do justice and love mercy.

In this hour of our trial, a word of information or of consolation from you would be a boon and a blessing.

Dorothea returned to work in the northern and middle states. The national population, including that of the indigent insane, had been steadily growing. She also resumed her inspection of almshouses and jails. She found that they had reverted to the deplorable conditions that had originally greeted her because these institutions were unable to cope with the growth of the population and the tide of immigration.

She wrote Mrs. Torrey: "It would seem that all my work is to be done over so far as the insane are concerned. Language is poor to describe the miserable state of these poor wretches in dungeon cells. I did not think I was to find here in this year 1868 such monstrous abuses."

Yet there were also encouraging results. On May 6, 1868, Professor Benjamin Silliman wrote her from New Haven: "It is just two years this month since you came here to move this matter, and now the first patients are in the New Hospital building. How much we all owe you for your timely aid, courage, and energy, without which this noble work would not have been undertaken, certainly for many years! And it was all done so quietly! The springs of influence were touched in a way which shows how possible it is to do great and noble things in public assemblies without a lobby or the use of money."

In one letter Dorothea wrote, "Tomorrow I go to the Northeastern district of the State of Pennsylvania to find a farm of 300 acres for the third hospital for which I have got an appropriation of $200,000."

The war had drained the nation's finances, dried up the "fountains of charity," as Marshall described it. The insane had increased, as expected, but a number of hospitals were abandoned because of rising costs. In 1867 Dorothea again assumed her duties as a self-appointed commissioner, inspecting jails, poorhouses, and institutions for the mentally ill. For the next fifteen years, she constantly traveled back and forth from New York to California and from Maine to Florida, visiting one institution after another, finding out what each needed.

In 1868 it was estimated that there were 54,285 mentally ill persons in the nation, 7,229 of whom were not provided for. There were fifty-four hospitals exclusively for mental illness and six under construction, Marshall reported. The Public Charities Commission of Pennsylvania announced that there were twice as many insane persons in prisons and poorhouses as when Dorothea made the appeal that resulted in the construction of the second state hospital in Harrisburg. Manacles, chains, and straitjackets, discarded years ago, were again in use.

Dorothea wrote Mrs. Torrey, "It would seem that all my work is to be done over so far as the insane are concerned."

One by one, she took up again the cause of the many asylums she had founded that now needed restoration and enlargement. She also worked to infuse into the minds of new legislators the need for the wiser treatment of the insane. From many an old asylum came grateful remembrances, such as that by John Harper, treasurer of the Dixmont Hospital in Pennsylvania, who wrote in 1871: "I trust when the warm weather comes, you will visit Dixmont and see for yourself what a monument for humanity has been erected and put into prosperous operation through your foresight and exertions. Do you remember the day in my room in the bank when you urged the establishment of a new rural hospital and the judge opposed you so bitterly? The judge was a man of great eloquence and influence, but you beat him, to his astonishment."

Earlier, on the occasion of presenting a portrait of Dorothea to the Dixmont Asylum by an unknown Philadelphia citizen, Harper wrote the donor: "You know, sir, in the olden time, each institution sacred to charity had its patron saint. The Dixmont Hospital, notwithstanding our Protestant and iconoclastic ideas, has a patroness whom we respect and love; indeed, who is canonized in our affections quite as strongly as were saintly ladies in the Medieval Age. The mission of 'our Lady' is to create those noble institutions which aid in the restoration of the dethroned reason, and Dixmont Hospital is one of the jewels which will adorn her crown hereafter."

Over the next few years Dorothea traveled from Maine to Texas, from New York to San Francisco, perpetually on the move. The asylums throughout the land became her terrain, her children. When she was seventy-five, in 1877, Dr. Charles F. Folsom of Boston wrote in his book *Diseases of the Mind* that her frequent visits to the institutions of the insane and her searching criticisms "constitute of themselves a better lunacy commission than would be likely to be appointed in many of our States." She could receive no higher praise for the work she had selected as her art.

But the inevitable infirmities of age started to take over. She became more silent and concentrated, more abrupt and imperative, "more the embodiment of habit than of the earlier spontaneity and enthusiasm which once irresistibly swept the legislatures of twenty States," according to Tiffany.

Her intellectual functioning, however, was as acute as ever. Nothing escaped her eyes, whether to be commended or criticized. She remained the organized conscience of the highest ideals of asylum management. The older members of the profession, who for years praised the value of her services, understood that her criticisms were dictated by an inner sense of justice and kindness, in Tiffany's words. But a number of the newer men in the most recent states objected to the quiet but authoritarian air she sometimes used. A few laughed at this "self-constituted lunacy commission in the person of a single aged woman."

The story was told of her entering an asylum where she called for a trial of the fire-extinguishing apparatus. It proved out of order and she uttered words of rebuke. Some of the younger doctors made fun of the "old lady" who believed she was saving the buildings from a conflagration. But Dorothea remembered asylums burning to the ground and scores of wretched inmates dying because the fire extinguishers had failed.

Mrs. Harriet C. Kerlin, wife of the superintendent of the institution for feeble-minded children at Elwyn, Pennsylvania, wrote of Dorothea:

> *Among our many visitors, there has never been one so ready to praise the good found, and so agreeably to reprove mistakes or failures. This may not always have been her characteristics, but surely we met only the gentle, considerate side of her nature, so that when Dr. Kerlin said, "Miss Dix, won't you come up to see where our teachers have rooms?" her reply, "Oh, no! doctor, I have never found any suffering among officers of an institution," was so frankly and half-wittily spoken, it carried no offensive sarcasm.*
>
> *If she were found at 5 o'clock A.M. in an unusual place, watching the early movements of our large family, her kindly manner of telling what she had seen, right or wrong, made us feel that sympathy with the superintendents prompted her desire for as perfect management as possible, and that no spirit of pleasure in spying out wrong had caused her unexpected early walk.*
>
> *She never gossiped about the weakness or faults of others. Her judgment was given with consideration of accompanying circumstances. Her language, voice, and manner were thoroughly gentle and lady-like, yet so strong was she in intelligence and womanhood that at times I ranked her alone, and above all other women.*

Some duly appointed state inspectors would beam graciously and ignorantly at what they thought the excellent conditions in which they found everything, drink a glass of wine in the medicinal room of the asylum, and then enjoy a lavish dinner. This was not Dorothea's way. She looked on her task not as child's play but an unpleasant ordeal at times.

She suffered a temporary setback when in spring 1870, at age sixty-eight she had to stop over in Louisville, Kentucky to shake off a cough that had become too overwhelming to neglect further. She spent the rest of the season indoors in Washington and then was taken to the Trenton hospital, desperately ill from "malaria in the most malignant form," as her physician declared, adding, "Her system has been saturated with it for years." She lingered for weeks at the hospital, swinging between life and death, according to Marshall, but was finally saved.

For a while she then carefully followed the doctor's orders not to take long journeys or work too hard. For the next few years, during her inspections and surveys, she appeared in a dark dress and shawl, carrying stuffed animals, clothes, toys, and magazines she had collected for patients in hospitals. When a fire in Boston left many Portuguese people homeless and destitute, she gathered food and clothing for them. But she spent more time "at home" in the Trenton hospital, the Pennsylvania hospital at Dixmont, named after her grandfather, and St. Elizabeth's, as the governmental hospital in Washington was now called.

It was difficult for her to admit she was growing old. It had been thirty-seven years since she had first visited the East Cambridge Jail. Now, early in 1878, she suffered two heartbreaking losses. First, her brother Joseph died, and shortly afterward, Anne passed away the evening before her seventy-ninth year. Both Dorothea's dearest kin and her oldest friend were gone. She had loved and frequently visited Joseph and his wife in their Boston home. Charles Wesley, her youngest brother, had died at sea in 1843, the year she presented her first *Memorial* to the Massachusetts Legislature.

Dorothea could at least take heart in the fact that she had started a revolution in the care of the poor, afflicted insane since the day she learned of them. From 13 institutions for the mentally ill in 1843, the number had risen to 123 in 1880, of which 75 were state owned; one was federal; and the others were the property of private corporations, churches, counties, and municipalities, according to Marshall's research. In founding more than thirty hospitals, Dorothea played an important part. There was still much work to be done, every hospital had a long waiting list, but at last society's conscience had been awakened.

The long-advocated special training for nurses in hospitals for the mentally ill had also become reality. Before Dorothea died, three states established training schools for nurses who would work in such hospitals.

The outcasts of the world were not easy to take care of, this she knew well. But she also realized that if they were treated humanely, they stood a chance of recovering sanity. This had been her staunch belief when she first decided to help them at age thirty-nine and it grew even stronger over the years.

Horace Mann, who had become a member of the House of Representatives and had always given her gracious support, died, as did William Rathbone, her supporter in England. Their deaths added to the grief she felt at the deaths of her brother and Anne.

Dorothea felt more alone than ever. But she had never allowed loneliness to stop her and did not intend to do so now

11

"A Kindly Thought on Her Who Bade This Fountain Flow"

First in Massachusetts, then throughout the United States, then in Europe, and finally in the Far East, Dorothea extended the rational and humane treatment of insanity as she became aware of one more continent that needed help in easing the suffering of disordered minds.

Several years before, Japan had sent its chargé d'affaires to Washington to represent that country's interests to the United States government. Dorothea, hearing of his arrival, went to Washington, sought to meet him, and held long and earnest meetings on how to help the insane in Japan. In Jugoi Arinori Mori, acknowledged as the foremost statesman of his country, she found someone of high intellectual ability and a deep sense of humanity.

After he returned home, he sent her a letter that illustrated once more the wisdom of one of her favorite maxims: "Sow beside *all* waters!" She received his letter from Tokyo, dated November 23, 1875: "My Dear Miss Dix,—During the long silence, do not think I have been idle about the matter in which you take so deep an interest. I have given the subject much of my time and attention, and have successfully established an asylum for the insane at Kyoto, and another in this city is being built and will soon be ready for its work of good. Other asylums will follow, too, and I ardently hope they will be the means of alleviating much misery."

She was delighted that two more asylums in a faraway country, with others likely to follow, would be added to the thirty-two she had already either founded outright or greatly enlarged. Unfortunately, Jugoi Arinori Mori would be assassinated a few years later by a fanatic.

In the last days of Dorothea's career, whenever any calamity occurred, such as fires that destroyed large portions of Chicago and Boston, she appeared on the spot carrying money she had collected from her many friends and learned at once where help was most needed. She also went to the rescue of animals; in a densely popu-lated section of Boston, for example, she set up a drinking fountain for draught horses after she noticed that they worked hard and looked tired and thirsty—no doubt recalling the many rides in her grandfather's carriage.

For many years she had exchanged letters with the famous Quaker poet, John Greenleaf Whittier, who sent her some of his poems before they were published. She had written him about the dramatic incident involving Barbara Frietchie, which he immortalized in verse. Now she asked him to send her the translation of an Arabic inscription cut on the curb of a drinking fountain in the Far East. This inscription had struck her as pertinent when he had quoted it on a previous occasion.

He wrote from Oak Knoll, "18th 8th Mo., 1879: My Dear Friend,—I cannot recall the Arabic inscription I referred to for the fountain, and have written one myself, taking it for granted that the fountain was to be thy gift, though thee did not say so.

"Such a gift would not be inappropriate for one who all her life has been opening fountains in the desert of human suffering,—who, to use Scripture phrase, has 'passed over the dry valley of Baca, making it a well.'" He signed the letter, "With love and reverence, thy friend, John G. Whittier."

His poem read:

> Stranger and traveler!
>   Drink freely and bestow
> A kindly thought on her
>   Who bade this fountain flow;
> Yet hath for it no claim
>   Save as the minister
> Of blessing in God's name.

Weary with fatigue after a journey through New England and New York inspecting almshouses, prisons, and hospitals when she was eighty-two, Dorothea went, in October 1881, to her "firstborn," the asylum in Trenton. She would never leave it.

The last glimpse of Dorothea outside the hospital was caught by George F. Jelly, superintendent of the McLean Hospital in Massachusetts, who wrote, shortly before Dorothea went to Trenton:

> *She arrived at my house in Boston after nightfall one bitter snowy winter evening. She seemed chilled to the marrow, and said she would go straight to bed. I offered her my assistance in mounting the staircase, but she declined every aid. The furnace draughts were opened for greater heat, a large fire was kept blazing in the grate of her bedroom, my wife piled five or six blankets on her, and I administered some warming drink.*
>
> *Spite of all she shivered with cold and would, I felt sure, succumb to pneumonia. She was on one of her tours of inspection, and had ordered the carriage to come for her in the early morning. Nothing could move her to change her plan, and when morning came she was up and ready to start. It was still a bitter snowstorm. I begged her at least to let me go with her to the station, for I feared she might die before she reached her destination. No! she would go alone. She was used to such things, she said, and, as soon as she had got through her work in New England, would go farther South, where she always became better soon.*

But once in Trenton, there would be no more exploring any parts of the country. The thousand-mile journeys from Halifax to Texas, from New York to San Francisco, had ended.

The managers of the New Jersey State Hospital, as it was now called, on hearing that Dorothea lay seriously ill in their hospital and might never be strong enough to leave it, called a meeting. They passed a unanimous vote inviting her to spend the rest of her days on the top floor of the first institution she had founded, as "its loved and revered guest."

Two large, comfortable apartments were assigned to her under the pediment of the Greek portico that formed the facade of the main building. She looked out on a view of parklike grounds, the open country, and the sweep of the Delaware River.

Her private resources would have served amply to keep her in comfort at a leading hotel the rest of her days, but she wished to end them as the honored guest of her "firstborn." Ever since her grandmother's death, for the past half century she had no home, but had lived from city to city. The asylums were her children and she was grateful that one of them now took her in, as a grown child might care for an elderly, ill parent.

She left her money in trust, the income to be devoted in perpetuity to charitable buildings, the "master passion of her life," in Tiffany's words.

Dorothea would occupy her hospital home for five years as she suffered a lasting exhaustion and the pain of the steadily advancing disease of which she died—ossification of the lining membranes of the arteries. Living within the walls of her room was difficult at first to this woman whose life had been an active one, for the most part. But no one heard her complain. "It is all right, it should be so," she said. "It is God's will, only it is hard to bear."

At no time since she was born had life seemed easy; it had always been a rather stern ordeal. She had learned words early to comfort herself. Now her Bible and collections of poetry eased her still-busy mind. She often included in letters she wrote friends in a trembling hand, cherished lines from hymns of all the ages.

Old friends did not forget her; letters from well-known persons arrived constantly. Many friends traveled across the country to spend an hour or two with her. Superintendents of asylums kept her informed of what went on in their world and sent her greetings of respect and love.

Dr. Kirkbride wrote on December 31, 1882: "In three hours

more, 1882 will belong to the past. May that which follows it bring to you, my most valued and honored friend, all the happiness that can come from a life devoted to good works and to the relief of the afflicted."

From Cincinnati came the greeting of her former pupil and life-long friend, Mrs. John Kebler: "I never think of you as grown old. You always come to me as I knew you first, crowned with rich brown hair, the like of which no one else ever had. Of all your pupils I am sure none loved you as I did and do. Few days of all my life have been unblessed by loving, grateful thoughts of the gracious, graceful teacher and friend. Always shall I connect with you, if I remain longer than you, that lovely hymn of Whittier, and my prayer shall be, —

> *Still, let thy mild rebukings stand*
> *Between me and the wrong,*
> *And thy dear memory serve to make*
> *My faith in goodness strong.*

Whittier sent a remembrance of cheer and consolation on May 6, 1882:

> *My Dear Friend,—I am glad to know that thou art with kind friends and as comfortable as possible under the circumstances. Thou has done so much for others that it is right for thee now, in age and illness, to be kindly ministered to. He who has led thee in thy great work of benevolence, will never leave thee nor forsake thee.*
>
> *With a feeling of almost painful unworthiness, I read thy overkind words as regards myself. I wish I could feel that I deserved them. But compared with such a life as thine, my own seems poor and inadequate. But none the less do I thank thee for thy generous appreciation.*
>
> *May the blessing of our Father in Heaven rest upon thee, dear friend! Believe me always and gratefully, thy Friend.*

Her old friend, the Reverend William G. Eliot of St. Louis, wrote: "We think and speak of you very often, and in spirit I spend many hours with you daily. Last night young Mr. Nichols, grandson of your old friend in Portland, was here, and we talked of you an hour. . . . After he left me, I wrote these lines before going to bed. They are a part of the truth, the whole of which cannot be told. . . . If love and gratitude and prayer could save you from all suffering and anxiety, no pain, nor loneliness of feeling would ever reach you."

He had written the poem:

Dear Sister, in thy lonely hours of suffering and pain,
Take comfort! The ten thousand prayers cannot ascend in
vain,

From hearts which thou hast comforted and homes
which thou has cheered,
And children, saved from ignorance, whose pathway thou
has cleared,
From loyal hearts and homes, wherever they are found,
In palaces and cottages, with peace and honor crowned.

Dear Sister, thou art not alone. God's angels hover near!
His presence is thy sure defense, then what has thou to
fear?
The "good fight" thou has nobly fought and truly "kept
the faith;"
The "crown" awaits thee, Sister dear, the "victory over
death;"
Take courage then, dear friend! The "prize" is almost
won;
Hark! 'Tis the Savior's voice we hear, "Servant of God,
well done!"

Similar testimonials of love and veneration from men and women throughout the country, as well as those on the other side of the Atlantic Ocean, rolled in. One letter came from a younger man in the battle of humanity, General S. C. Armstrong, who fought bravely for the preservation of the Union. As soon as peace arrived, he "beat his sword into a plowshare and his spear into a pruning hook," working to help the freed, formerly ignorant and degraded Negroes become self-respecting American citizens.

In General Armstrong's first efforts to reduce the chaos and anarchy of the region around Hampton, Virginia, he found no more staunch a friend or wise adviser than Dorothea. He wrote: "You are one of my heroes. My ideal is not one who gives the flush and strength of youth in good work,—for who can help doing so when a chance opens! He is a traitor who declines the chances, just as is he who doesn't fight for his country when it needs him, and he can possibly go. But you kept to the field long past your best days. Your grit and resolve have been wonderful. Faithfully yours, S. C. Armstrong."

Her friend, the famous Dr. Daniel Hack Tuke, made a special trip to Trenton to see her when he visited America to obtain material for his book, *The Insane in the United States and Canada*, telling her once again how much he admired her.

But her afflictions increased as she became deaf, her sight was impaired, and her memory often faded. Even aged and suffering, Dorothea did not want to die. "I think even lying on my bed, I can still do something," she said.

As long as strength lasted, it remained her custom to sit during the declining hours of sunlight at her windows, looking out at the beautiful landscape and watching the patients walk the paths.

The end occurred on the evening of July 17, 1887. She was eighty-five years old. During the past month, she had steadily weakened. She begged her dear friend Dr. John E. Ward, the current director, to avoid the use of anodynes, but just to tell her when the last hour was near.

Dr. Ward was sitting at the teatable when a nurse ran over to report that Dorothea was sinking. He ran up the stairs and threw open the door to her rooms. As his eyes fell on Dorothea, she breathed her final, quiet sigh, Tiffany reported.

She was buried in the height of summer heat in Mount Auburn Cemetery in Cambridge at the foot of a small slope. Just above her lay her close friend Dr. William Ellery Channing, who believed in her as a teacher and helped her recover from her first illness by taking her out of the cold winter in Boston to St. Croix. He had taught her that "Man's work is mankind." Over her grave flew the American flag and the standard of the Corps of Army Nurses. Her gravestone bore only her name: Dorothea L. Dix.

Her longtime friends Dr. Ward, Dr. Charles H. Nichols, and Horace A. Lamb stood by the grave as she was buried. Later Dr. Nichols wrote Dr. Tuke in England: "Thus has died and been laid to rest in the most quiet, unostentatious way the most useful and distinguished woman America has yet produced."

Two years after Dorothea's death, *The York* (England) *Home Journal* of September 11, 1889, carried an article reminiscing about her character and career. It was written by a friend of earlier years, Mrs. S. G. Miller, who lived in Princeton, New Jersey. Mrs. Miller described Dorothea's last days in her asylum home.

She started by saying she

> *accidentally met an oldtime friend from Washington who mentioned a recent visit to Miss Dix in the Trenton asylum. Eagerly inquiring about her, I learned that she was a confirmed invalid, occupying apartments in the Insane Asylum at Trenton, which had been given to her by the State of New Jersey in acknowledgment of her agency in securing the creation of the building. At the earliest moment I went over to see her, sending up my card, with much misgiving as to her memory of me. Immediately I was taken to her rooms in the tower. She was glowing in her welcome: "I told them to bring you right up, for I was so impatient to see my friend that I would not wait a minute."*
>
> *She was propped up in bed and greatly altered. I said, "You should be at the pains, Miss Dix, to arrange that you go down to posterity in that beautiful portrait of you in the Atheneum at Boston." A smile of satisfaction brightened her face at the suggestion; and I was amused to see that even the good and great, and strong and old, possessed in common with their weaker sisters, a keen relish of a gentle insinuation of personal beauty.*
>
> *It was evident to me that her helplessness did not extend either to her head or hands, for soon I saw that her warmest interest was still flowing in its long-accustomed channel, and that from her sick room lines of communication ran in every direction to the outside world. She spoke of the gift made to her of her rooms with much gratification.*

Her sense of home seemed wholly centered in them. The cosey little bedroom opened into a small, bright parlor, from the windows of which was an exquisite view of the grounds and distant landscape.

"Are you strong enough," I asked her on one occasion, "to use your pen as in former times?" Summoning the nurse, she had some loose sheets handed to me, saying, "I wrote these and had them printed by the Indian boys at Hampton; but I can't hold lines long in my memory." They were short hymns, and her difficulty was to frame a verse and hold it in mind until she could get it on paper either by her own hand or that of another. . . .

She was unfeignedly interested in good work done by other hands, and her manner in discussing it, that of the fellow-laborer, not of the master-workman. I never descried the faintest soupçon of such assumption nor did I ever detect any personal ambition in her great work. She never sought notoriety. Not even in the seclusion of her last years, when it would have been so natural for her to entertain me with the exciting scenes of her previous history, did she ever drag in her past enterprises and successes. Present work seemed to fill her mind, not her former triumphs.

Of course her friendliness extended to my family. I took my daughters to see her, and under the impulse of her ruling passion she inquired what schemes of usefulness entered into their young lives. One of them detailed to her the effort she was making to benefit the children in her church. On subsequent visits, months afterward, Dorothea asked how it went on. I pictured its progress with some warmth, she listening sympathizingly and now and then nodding approvingly, when she suddenly exclaimed with a beaming smile, "I know she would like to have her fingers in my purse; now wouldn't she?" I promptly declined any gift, telling her my daughter already had objects enough of her own to prosecute; but Dorothea would not be denied, and a crisp new bill so large that I protested against it, was sent with the message "that of all the agencies of charity the school was the most hopeful."

*It is a mistake that age has power to cast out the evil
instincts of human nature. It often intensifies them. Anger
and bitterness scowl along the twilight of many a brilliant
career, as the dark clouds gather upon the evening horizon
of some exquisite day. With Miss Dix this was not so; her
heated, excited day merged into a quiet, peaceful close. In
the full tide of work she had been called imperious and
arbitrary. These traits may have been necessary; certainly,
they were powerful aids in the accomplishment of her
splendid designs; but as the night drew on, her character
mellowed, and all that was most lovable in her nature
appeared as her life slowly faded away.*

*She suffered at times agonies of pain, and her ability at
self-entertainment lessened rapidly in the last year. She
had become extremely deaf, her sight also was much impaired, and in her increasing bodily feebleness I imagine
that her well-stored memory, from which she had drawn
so largely for her comfort and refreshment, now often
deserted her. Kind friends sought to aid her failing senses
by the best help that science could supply, but in vain.*

*It was pitiful to have her say to me, "Try to put this tube
in my ear so as not to pain, and yet allow me to hear what
you say." And of her eyes, too, she said in a sort of despair-
ing attempt at cheerfulness, "I do not think it right to get
such numbers of spectacles that nobody else can use, and
which do me no good."*

*I saw her only a few months before her death, when
she had become so weak as to allow me to stay only half
an hour. Feeble as she was, however, with that singular
thoughtfulness for others which never left her, she endeavored to entertain the daughter I had brought with
me. As the interview wore on it became evident to me that
she wished to say something confidential, and at her
suggestion I tried to manoeuver the faithful nurse out of
hearing.*

*Failing ignominiously, I said, "Oh, never mind now;
tell me when I can come again." "Ah yes, if I am here; if I
am here." "Oh," I replied, quite too warmly I feared, to
meet her wishes, for I thought death would be welcomed*

> by her,—*"Oh, I hope you will be here for many a year to come."*
>
> *She started up with agitated eagerness and said, with wild excitement, "My dear friend, if you hope that, pray for it: pray that I may be here. I think even lying on my bed I can still do something." She fell back upon her pillow exhausted, whilst I, moved and surprised beyond measure, sat down that she might have time to recover her composure. I then rose to go. She threw her arms around me, saying with unwonted tenderness, "O darling!" and I had parted with my old friend forever.*

Tiffany pointed out that the exclamation, "O darling!" occurred again and again in the broken, fragmentary letters she wrote close friends at this time. It proved, he said, "what a world of tenderness underlay that self-controlled, amantine character with which she had fronted the world in her long warfare for the outcast and despised."

Helping the helpless was her goal. She had eased their pain in more than twenty states stretching over half the continent, from the pines and maples of Newfoundland to the palmettos of Louisiana. She had also lessened the torture of the indigent insane in Europe and Japan. Dorothea had spent almost her entire life putting into action a belief that has mitigated the misery of hundreds of thousands of men and women.

Why was she the one to take on this superhuman task? What in her life had caused her to concentrate with such fierce dedication on those whose minds had gone astray and could not help themselves back to normalcy?

12

WHY DOROTHEA TURNED SAVIOR

What drove Dorothea to reject a life of marriage and child rearing, the way most women lived at that time, to devote her days to relieving the misery of the mentally disturbed? Why did she champion their cause ardently for so many years, over and above all other concerns?

Underneath Dorothea's surface calm she hid a childhood rage she never allowed to rise to the surface. Like most children, she buried her outbursts so her parents would love her. Children's deepest fear is of being abandoned by their parents, for they then believe no one will take care of them and they will die.

Her belief that she could go it alone hid many feelings of being forsaken and included a devastating fear of men. She had seen her father attack her mother in an alcoholic fury, and this was her image of a "man"—a destructive creature who might one day kill the woman he married.

She also had to feel strange in having a mother who was twice as old as her father, whereas all the other girls' mothers were far younger than the men they married. Her family was different, freakish. She must have often felt an outcast, like the mentally ill she spent most of her lifetime trying to help.

Unconsciously, she copied her mother in a physical sense, falling continually ill after she started teaching and never truly feeling healthy from then on. Little girls use their mothers as their image of themselves—who else is there to learn from? Dorothea worked day and night to establish her two schools and injured her lungs because of the lack of sleep. Her mother often spent most of the day in bed, and for a while Dorothea did, too, until she gave up the rigors of teaching two separate classes after losing a lung. Even with this handicap, the strong spirit within would not give up, and she would live to be eighty-five, working hard until she was eighty-one, then falling ill. In many ways she refused to be like her mother but her constant illnesses mirrored her mother's misery.

To understand her steadfast choice of fighting for the proper treatment of the indigent mentally ill, we need to be aware of her early relationships to her mother, father, grandmother, and grandfather during what are called the "formative years" of her life. The first three years set the stage for all our later behavior. How Dorothea's parents treated her during this time and how she consciously and unconsciously took in their wishes, attitudes, and goals fashioned her future.

Her father, Joseph Dix, was an unhappy man who wanted to become a minister instead of the physician his doctor-father wished him to be. Joseph entered Harvard at seventeen, but within a year angered his father by forsaking the family's Calvinistic worship. Instead, Joseph insisted he wanted to be a minister like his idol, the preacher Charles Wesley, who wandered the streets giving solace to the poor. When Joseph's parents showed their disgust at this wish, he started to drink in Boston taverns and never gave up the desire for alcohol the rest of his life.

At eighteen, in his second year at Harvard, he met Mary Bigelow, who was nearly thirty-six. They fell in love and married at once, in spite of his parents' strong objections that he was tying himself to a woman old enough to be his mother. Joseph was then expelled from Harvard, which had the rule no student could marry and remain in college. From then on, he preached in the streets, as his idol Wesley did, handing out tracts on salvation of the soul.

We might also wonder about a woman who married an obviously emotionally disturbed young man half her age, who could never support her. It was as if she married a child whom she would have to take care of but was unable to do so because of the bereft, angry child within her.

Dorothea's childhood, as described by Tiffany, was one of depression and emotional pain. She thought her father lived "with a torment in his head." She saw him suffering "spells" as he retreated to another world at times, wandering around as though he had lost his mind.

Her elderly mother was sick in a different way from that of her father. Her mother did not touch alcohol, but seemed unavailable to her daughter and two sons as she lay in bed day after day. It is no accident that Dorothea as an adult was often downed by crippling sickness. Daughters emulate their mothers in many ways. Dorothea would later copy parts of her father as she gave solace to the poor—not through dedication to God, as her father had done, but as her lifelong task of complete dedication to the out-of-their-minds men and women.

Joseph loved his firstborn, he taught her at a very early age to read and write and asked her to help distribute his religious pamphlets. From him she absorbed a sense of the vast need to aid the unfortunate poor.

Dorothea felt acutely her grandparents' dislike of her mother and her father's way of living. Since Joseph had little or no income, his parents paid for the upkeep of his family wherever they lived. Her grandmother advised her grandfather, according to Tiffany, to place the newly married couple as far away from them as he could because she was ashamed of them. Dr. Dix, who had bought land in Maine, hoping to become even wealthier, sent his son and wife to live there. He hoped Joseph would help sell some of the property, but Joseph worked only on his ministerial duties.

Since her mother was usually ill, Dorothea early became the caretaker of her two younger brothers, as in a way she also was of the indigent insane. At a time when most little girls possessed or playful thoughts, Dorothea was well on her way to being a substitute mother. As she later said sadly, "I never knew childhood." At fifteen she was still playing the caretaker, as she would almost until the day she died.

While growing up, she heard her mother and father quarrel constantly and saw her father strike her mother at times when he was drunk. Her parents' relationship did not give her a happy portrait of marriage, which she always feared. She must have also sometimes felt that she had two sets of parents—her mother and father, who were literally her poor, bickering parents, and her grandparents, who were the wealthy elite who did not fight, at least openly.

As an adult Dorothea was extremely erudite, often poetic, but very shy. Tiffany described a "quick flushing of her face whenever she was addressed." But she would not give an inch when she fought to help the poverty-stricken, emotionally disturbed. She eagerly sought the company of powerful legislators who could further her cause and who seemed to accept her fully, as her grandfather had during the first seven years of her life. She never allowed anything to jeopardize that cause, not even during the Civil War, though she thought the South's refusal to free the black slaves was inexcusable.

Her quiet, contained voice, her attractive face, and her soulful blue eyes, attracted important men who believed in her goals. She convinced these men of the need to help the indigent insane, following her recovery from the illness that cost her one lung and crippled her for five years until she was thirty-nine. During this quiet period, she decided to give up teaching and help others in a different way.

Her first visit to East Cambridge Jail, where she found the emotionally ill housed underground in dark pits, provided the answer to how she would help those who could not help themselves, as she witnessed the vicious cruelties to which they were subjected. From then on, she was driven by one goal—to relieve their misery.

A large share of Dorothea's strength no doubt came from the one person in her early life from whom she received constant love and attention. She basked in her grandfather's desire to see her as often as he could. Her grandfather spent much of his time with her when she visited Dix Mansion, kissed her goodbye tenderly when she left join her distraught parents. She was only seven years old when lost him completely, and she must have deeply mourned his death forever after. We do not ever totally recover from our early emotional deprivations.

In contrast to her grandfather, who had loved her openly, her grandmother never showed outward signs of love. She seemed a rigid, dominating woman after Dorothea moved into Dix Mansion at age twelve. To Dorothea, Dix Mansion must have been a palace, though a palace without love. Dorothea's mother and father now lived in Vermont, and there is no mention in Tiffany's book of her ever seeing them again.

When she was fourteen, Dorothea was sent to live four years with her grandmother's sister in Worcester, ostensibly to learn how to dress as a fashionable young lady and to find some man who would eventually marry her. It was there that her second-cousin Edward fell in love with her and helped her establish her first school for little girls. Dorothea would never marry, undoubtedly because of her parents' unhappy marriage that she had endured as a child.

In one way, she never had a home. It was as though she cried out for one as she undertook the real work of her lifetime, traveling from city to city, state to state, nation to nation, establishing "homes" for the poverty-stricken men and women who seemed mindless. Her "home," in her fantasy, became the one she built, time after time, for the world's troubled souls. She valued such temporary homes far above any steadfast one, as though they all made up for her lack of one home during childhood.

She could establish no lasting home for herself. She had seen her parents unable to do so as they moved from state to state, village to village. She, too, became peripatetic, traveling from place to place, as though pulled by an inexorable string.

Today we take for granted our mental hospitals for the indigent in every state of the nation. We call them retreats for the "emotionally disturbed," rather than for the "pauper insane." It was Dorothea Lynde Dix who lifted their status from that of wounded beasts who were brutalized, chained, thrown food as though they were vicious dogs, and left to freeze in the cold, to that of troubled mortals who could be helped to regain their senses as they received understanding care that helped them reach the roots of their inner disturbances.

Dorothea was years ahead of Freud in knowing that such help was the only way to restore sanity to the deeply depressed. It took a lo woman who campaigned from the age of thirty-nine to the day she died at eighty-five, to champion in our country a cause that would spread across the world.

As with any important act, there are many reasons, some conscious, others unconscious, why Dorothea chose to further the understanding of those who had temporarily lost their minds. For one, she followed in the footsteps of her loving grandfather, who drove her around in his carriage, talking to her in "his strong and racy way," as Tiffany described it. Tiffany believed that her grandfather stood out "as the one bright spot in her earliest memories, implanting in her mind a lifelong admiration for his robust and picturesque qualities." He undoubtedly imbued her, as he talked to her, with the feeling that she was important to him, that he was proud of her. She thus later in life felt at ease with men at the top, who quickly admired her for her outstanding, new ideas.

Dorothea unfortunately always carried with her, as her mother had so openly revealed, a lasting illness that would at times cripple her. But she also had a strong will to live, emanating in great part from the love her grandfather had shown her. Of the many asylums for troubled souls that she established, she permitted only one to be associated with her name. This was Dixmont Hospital in Pennsylvania, named in tribute to her grandfather, founder of the town of Dixmont, Maine, which he had once owned, where she was born and he died and was buried.

Dorothea unconsciously tried to be the savior of her mother and father as she worked to rescue the "family" of the indigent insane. Buried deep beneath her awareness of this outward task was her wish to save not only her parents but her brothers and herself.

She wrote at the close of 1856 to Dr. J.M. Cleaveland of the Hudson River State Hospital in New York: "It is truly sorrowful to find so much suffering through neglect, ignorance and mismanagement, but I hope for better things at no distant time. The weather has been severe and stormy, but in proportion as my own discomforts have increased, my conviction of the necessity of search into the wants of the friendless and afflicted has deepened."

Then occurred the very important words—ones that gave away her deepest feelings and caused her to become famous—as she spoke of the "friendless and afflicted": "If I am cold, they are cold; if I am weary, they are distressed; if I am alone, they are abandoned."

This sentence said it all. "If I am alone, they are abandoned," told of her feelings about the poverty-stricken inmates but on a deeper level applied to how she had felt as a girl about her mother, her father, and her two younger brothers.

Dorothea grew up feeling, as her life proves, that she had to be the savior of her family, to take care of those who could not take care of themselves, so that they and she would survive. She early realized that her often "out of this world" father and her "always sick" mother were not capable of caring for their children or themselves.

Her father's drinking proved this, as did his refusal to find work. A psychiatrist would point out that, in one sense, Joseph had married his mother, since his wife was actually twice his age, and he would later feel guilty about this forbidden act and drink even more heavily to try to obliterate his guilt. Turning to religion so ardently became a way of asking perpetual forgiveness from God.

Dorothea proved that she could go it alone; her accomplishments for a woman of her time were unbelievable. At fifteen she became a schoolteacher and remained one until she fell ill in her early thirties. When she was thirty-nine, she started collecting money to house the poor insane, and for the rest of her life continued to create hospitals and spread her mission not only throughout this country but throughout England, Ireland, other European nations, and Japan. She also served for four years as first superintendent of nurses for the Northern army during the Civil War and then returned to founding more hospitals.

In Dorothea's arduous work to help the world understand the need for tender, loving care of the indigent insane lay her early, powerful, hidden childhood plea for someone to take care of her and her family. Her father's bouts with insanity, his inability to provide financially for a wife, daughter, two sons, and himself, and her mother's constant sickliness aroused Dorothea's early fervent wish that her parents had been "normal" people who could truly love and care for her.

Dorothea's intense, driving need to spend her life quietly but doggedly seeking help for the poor insane was the cause she championed as she unconsciously told the world, as we all do in one way or another, of her own and her family's misery.

Dorothea lived out, in a way that would eventually benefit the world, her unconscious dream of a wish that all indigent insane persons—men, women, and children—should have the chance to be cured in a fit, caring atmosphere so the conflicts that had driven them crazy could be understood as they regained their sanity.

To Dorothea's satisfaction, she removed mountains of misery. She saw the fulfillment of her early dreams. She created hospitals in which deeply troubled men and women, some of them violent, were helped to cope with their fantasies and fears.

It was no surprise that her ideas were accepted so swiftly wherever she went, on whatever continent she appeared. Everyone sensed she was right, that to cripple further those who were mentally unbalanced was to act inhuman. The goal of civilization was to help the emotionally crippled, not to increase their misery, hoping they would die.

Our world today owes the gallant, subtly brilliant Dorothea Lynde Dix, whose emotional life was filled with deep unhappiness but whose mind held a strength that survived eighty-five years, a great and lasting tribute. She paved the way for lifesaving help for those who dared not, indeed were unable to, ask for it.

She did perhaps more than anyone else has done to show the world the meaning of the word "humanity"—kindness, mercy, sympathy, and understanding of those who cannot afford to pay for the help that cures. For Dorothea, "not in the winning of laurels, but in the succor of human misery, lay the dominating purpose of her life," as Tiffany wrote. And, as Tiffany noted, she was "a woman of great pride and dignity of character, fully conscious, too, of the immensity of the work she had achieved on two continents, yet she shrank in utter aversion from what seemed to her the degradation of mere public notoriety."

She would never allow any publicity about herself. When Mrs. Sarah J. Hale, working in 1851 on a book *Lives and Characters of Distinguished Women*, asked Dorothea for data from which to write an account of her career, Dorothea replied:

> *I feel it right to say to you frankly that nothing could be undertaken which would give me more pain and serious annoyance, which would so trespass on my personal rights, or interfere more seriously with the real usefulness of my mission. I am not ambitious of nominal distinctions, and notoriety is my special aversion.*
>
> *My reputation and my services belong to my country. My history and my affections are consecrated to my friends. It will be soon enough when the angel of the last hour shall have arrested my labors to give their history and their results. This period cannot be many years distant.*

She would live thirty-six more years. Except for the last five, she kept active. Even when she had to remain in her room day after day in the Trenton, New Jersey, hospital, which she had named her "firstborn child," she kept active, writing letters and poetry, welcoming friends who visited her, including General John A. Dix of New York (no relation to her) and Alexander Randall of Annapolis, Maryland.

Mr. Randall had far earlier, in 1880 before she entered the hospital, begged her not to let her life story die with her. He asked her to dictate the leading incidents of her career to him. She wrote Mr. Randall on May 10, 1880: "I can not, my valued friend, bring into order suitably for a brief memoir any written details that seem to me fitly to convey to any reader what cannot be realized, because there is no relative standard of contrast or comparison. The whole of my years, from the age of ten to the present, differ essentially from the experience and pursuits of those around me."

Tiffany pointed out that "in no hour of the confidential intimacy could she be induced to unlock the silence which to the very end of always remained the memory of its bitterness."

Those early days held much pain, that we know. Dorothea had a brilliant mind, like her father, who taught her to love words and books. She further developed her mind by reading the classics and teaching, but part of her longed to help the tortured souls of the world who, like her father, sometimes left reality to create an inner world of their own that felt less destructive.

We might also venture the guess that Joseph, one of seven sons, thought his parents had wanted a second daughter. Caught in this dilemma, he chose not to be an active male like his father, who as a physician worked hard and made money, but a peaceful, wandering preacher who cared only about the minds of men, not the manly deeds that brought fame and fortune—in other words, he acted more like a woman.

When we are deeply unhappy from childhood on, one way of escaping misery is to regress to dreams and wishes that take us out of what we feel is tortured reality. The emotionally troubled person often resorts to this when life becomes too unbearable. Dorothea understood the burdens borne by the insane, set about to help such stricken souls recover by championing their rights to an understanding of what drove them to such deep despair.

Tiffany said that he was under a "great obligation" to Dr. Daniel Hack Tuke for a letter dated "Hanwell, England, August, 1888," containing Dr. Tuke's memories of the time he spent with Dorothea. Dr. Tuke wrote that his reminiscences of her visit in 1855, during which she was his guest at York for several weeks "were exceedingly vivid as to the general impression left upon the memory," but that he regretted to say that the lapse of about thirty-three years "has to some extent obliterated the details, interesting and fruitful in result as they were, in the cause of the insane which she had so much at heart."

He described her as

> *very much out of health . . . confined to bed for some days, but the indomitable energy with which she pursued her mission was extraordinary. She visited most of the insti-*

tutions for the insane about York. . . . There is not a doctor in Scotland, at the present day, interested in the welfare of the insane and in the splendid asylums now in operation in that country, who would not acknowledge the profound debt of gratitude due to Miss Dix for her courage, her pertinacity, and her judicious advice.

You ask me to indicate the salient features of Miss Dix's character as they struck me when I knew her. She told me of having in the early part of her life intended to live mainly to herself, to enjoy literature and art without any higher aims, and of having discovered that this was a fatal mistake. She then resolved to devote her energies to the good of man and this seems to me the pivot on which her future career revolved.

The lines of one of her country-women might seem to have been especially composed to describe the change which came over Miss Dix:—
I slept and dreamt that life was beauty,
I woke, and found that life was duty.

He also said that

her long sustained exertions, undertaken from the highest motives, mark the untiring and irrepressible energy and fortitude which more especially struck me during our personal acquaintance. That these qualities must have exerted enormous influence in inducing others—especially young physicians —to engage in the humane treatment of the insane can easily be understood. . . .

The refinement and intrinsic gentleness of Miss Dix had much to do with the esteem and affection entertained for her, because they disarmed the criticism and opposition which were not unnaturally excited when a woman entered the public arena, and was expected to commit injudicious and emotional acts, however well-intentioned they might be. But Miss Dix's enthusiasm was based on actual facts and undeniable abuses, while the remedies she proposed were those which commended themselves to the best men engaged in the treatment of the insane in the United States.

He ended his letter: "I will only say, in conclusion, that in whatever other department Miss Dix may have earned the gratitude of mankind, in that of the proper care and humane treatment of the insane (not the so-called nonrestraint system which she did not accept) she ought to be regarded as the patron saint of every hospital for this class established through her instrumentality, as an angel of mercy, not only in her own, but in other lands, and therefore held in everlasting remembrance on both sides of the Atlantic as one worthy of double honor."

Information about Dorothea's personal life, Tiffany wrote, was scarce. He explained: "Except for a few brief accounts of her career, printed in magazines, read before private clubs, or inserted in encyclopedias, no real information is to be had about her. Occasionally she speaks of her deepest feelings to her long-time friend, Anne, her only confidant."

After asking why the majority of the "present" generation (referring to the late 1800s) knows "little or nothing" of her remarkable achievements, Tiffany answered, "It was from no lack of pressure on the part of admirers and venerators of the character and work of so exceptional a woman that this came about. The invincible obstacle lay in her own positive refusal to permit anything to be written of her."

He added, "Not in the winning of laurels, but in the succor of human misery, lay the dominating purpose of her life. A woman of great pride and dignity of character, fully conscious, too, of the immensity of the work she had achieved on two continents, she yet shrank in utter aversion from what seemed to her the degradation of mere public notoriety."

Tiffany believed that two equally strong, but totally contrasted natures lay in her: "the one the outcome of a sensitive, suffering temperament, instinctively seeking to shield itself from gall or wound; the other born of the fortitude of a martyr in fronting danger, loneliness, and obloquy, in championing the cause of the friendless and 'ready to perish.' To all this must be added a depth of self-abnegating religious faith which made her life one long struggle to prostrate a spirit naturally proud and imperious at the footstool of God, in the lowly cry, 'Not unto me, not unto me, but unto Thy Name be the praise!' "

Tiffany reported that toward the end of her life, helpless with illnesses, Dorothea made faltering attempts to put her papers in order. By then, however, she was too feeble for such a task, and the papers were left in confusion. Shortly before she died, she gave to her trusted friend and executor, Horace A. Lamb of Boston, her full consent, if he wished, for the papers to be used in the preparation of a memoir of her life and work.

Unfortunately, in what must be regarded "as a mistaken sense of the duty of self-effacement," Tiffany pointed out, "she had previously issued positive commands to her many friends to destroy her private letters. A few of these friends happily refused to obey the injunction, and to their pious care for her memory is it alone due that any vivid picture can at this date be drawn of her."

The world can only be thankful that Dorothea existed and worked so valiantly for the rights of those who could not speak for themselves. She was the pioneer supreme in the field of mental health for those who could not afford to pay for the chance to feel "human," probably for the first time in their lives.

Dorothea Lynde Dix created her own mission in life. It proved an unusual one, for women of that time rarely left their husbands and children for the world of work, and those who chose not to marry lived with their parents, brothers, or sisters, not daring to embark on a career.

Part of Dorothea may have regretted that she never married and had a family, but, as she said, the hospitals were her "children." They were children of a different sort, but children who provided understanding and love to those whose sanity had been affected by cruel parents. In a sense, Dorothea's parents had been cruel to her, driven by their own deep despair, but they also had provided her with enough inner strength so she could eventually give the mentally needy the chance to become emotionally free.

She waged a new kind of battle, gaining a victory that meant the bestowing of kindness and understanding on those who were formerly thrown into dark jails and almshouses, chained, beaten, and always insufficiently fed.

Dorothea Lynde Dix proved a new kind of heroine, a woman who donated her time and energy to convince legislatures to pass laws that meant hope for the mentally ill.

In her quiet, effective way, she overcame obstacles that were herculean. She deserves lasting honor.

INDEX

ABOUT THE
AUTHORS

Charles Schlaifer, as vice-president of 20th Century-Fox Film Corporation, was responsible for the worldwide presentation in 1948 of *The Snake Pit*. From 1947 on, in addition to his other work, including the presidency of his own advertising agency, Mr. Schlaifer lobbied the United States Congress and the executive branch to create and fund the National Institute of Mental Health and created and co-chaired the National Mental Health Committee. For fifteen years he was chairman of New York State's Facilities Development Corporation.

Among his many contributions to the mental health field are these: Member of the Advisory Council to the Surgeon General of the United States for the National Institute of Mental Health, secretary-treasurer of the Congressional Joint Commission on Mental Health, and secretary and treasurer of the Joint Commission on Mental Health of Children. He was co-author of the book *Action for Mental Health*, which set forth nationwide guidelines for improving treatment of the mentally ill and co-author of *Crisis in Child Mental*

Health. He is also an honorary fellow of the American Psychiatric Association and of the American Orthopsychiatric Association.

Lucy Freeman, author of sixty-seven books, started as a news reporter on *The New York Times*, where she established the mental health beat. She is best known for *Fight Against Fears*, the story of her psychoanalysis, which has sold more than a million copies and is still in print after thirty-nine years. Two of her books have been television features. *Betrayal* was shown in 1982 on NBC, the story of a young woman who sued a New York psychiatrist for using sex as therapy. *Psychologist With Gun*, written with Dr. Harvey Schlossberg, was the basis of the 1984 television series *Jessie* on ABC.

Ms. Freeman has written books on true crime, including *"Before I Kill More,"* the story of a young Chicago murderer, believed to be the first "whydunit." She is past president of the Mystery Writers of America. Her latest book, with Dr. Herbert S. Strean, was published in April 1991, *Our Wish to Kill: The Murder In All Our Hearts.* Among her biographies are *The Story of Anna O,* the woman Freud said led him to his psychoanalytic theories.